Victorious Faith

Richard Wurmbrand

Victorious Faith

Titza Mihalache
1510 164th St. #4
San Leandro, CA 94578

I gratefully acknowledge my indebtedness to Mrs Ellen Oblander who edited my rough English with sympathetic delicacy.—R.W.

VICTORIOUS FAITH

Mozart, at the age of four, when asked how he composed music, answered, "I just put together little notes that like each other."

This is what I have done, too. Thoughts and stories gathered according to their own affinities have been put on paper. That is all.

ONCE upon a time, there was a prince who received a very rare and beautiful bird. He named it Twee-Twee and placed it in a golden cage. But the poor creature was not impressed by the gold. It pleaded for freedom, but the prince liked it too much to part with it. Then Twee-Twee begged him at least to visit her relatives in the forest and tell them that, though captive, she was still alive.

The prince went and told them. At once, Twee-Twee's sister fell to the ground, and the prince realized that she had been killed by the grief of knowing freedom-loving Twee-Twee was in a cage. Sad at heart, he returned and told Twee-Twee the sad news that her sister had died. Immediately Twee-Twee collapsed in the same way at the bottom of the cage. The prince then took the poor bird out of the cage and threw her through the window. What would be the purpose in keeping her when she was dead? In a flash, Twee-Twee flew away and, from a tree, chirped, "What you thought was bad news was a lesson. By pretending to have died, my sister taught me the way to escape."

Nobody can exhaust the sense of Jesus' death on Calvary. But the wise have always taught by deeds. Through dying by his own will at the age of 33, young and full of power, Jesus gave us a lesson on how to handle the problems of life. Die to them!

Does sin attract you? Would you commit sin if you were dead? Surely not. Then drop dead! The world wishes to involve you in its race toward destruction. Be dead to it! Religions wish to force your life into the mould or a law. Die to the law! Jesus died to sin, the world, and the law. Because of this, He lives. You, the captive, can become free by following His example. Are problems haunting you? Be impassive to them, as if you were dead.

Learn from the story of the bird which obtained its freedom.

The purpose of this book is to show the way of liberty.

*   *

*

My book is not the expression of opinions and sentiments of a man. I hate stuffy—as well as inspired—sermons in which clergymen express *their* views and *their* standpoints. I also hate political rallies at which good or bad opinions are expressed. I would prefer that nobody open his mouth unless he knows a truth, an objective truth.

In times of old, there were men among the Jews called prophets, who, when they wrote or when they spoke, began with the words, "Thus spake the Lord".—

I write the present book with the full assurance that I am only a voice. Through me, God Himself speaks.

Some will laugh at this assertion at the beginning of a book.

I always like it when people laugh, even at me. Laughter is healthy. Doctors recommend it. There is so little reason to laugh in this world. Why should people not laugh at me? Take it as foolishness if you like, but through this my book, God speaks to you.

How do I know that? Is not God Someone other than me, Someone totally different from me? My means of communication with Him can sometimes work well, but can also be troubled: I might misunderstand Him.

Jesus on the cross cried, "Eli, Eli" (the Hebrew words for "My God, My God"). Those beneath the cross believed they heard the name of the prophet Elijah. Such misunderstandings are daily occurrences.

How then can I have the assurance that what I, Richard Wurmbrand, write is exactly what God wishes me to convey? How did the prophets know?

* *

*

A great confusion of spheres has taken place. The sphere of grammar and the sphere of religion are different from each other. Every pupil in school, who, when asked to conjugate a verb, replies that God is love and that whosoever believes in Him is born of God, will get a bad mark, even if the teacher is religious. Religion has no place in an examination on grammar.

But neither has grammar any say in religion. In the sphere of practical life we have to conjugate verbs, and for this we need personal pronouns. We have to distinguish between properties: between *my* house, *my* book, *my* wife, and that belonging to another. And so we have to use "I", "you", and "he". But please leave pronouns in the realm of grammar, to which they belong: do not introduce them into religion!

When Jesus Christ met Saul of Tarsus, a great persecutor of the Christians, on the road to Damascus, He asked him, "Saul, Saul, why persecutest thou *Me*?" Saul could have answered truthfully, "I never persecuted *you*. I persecuted your disciples". But Jesus, though omniscient, does not know that He and His disciples are different persons. He feels *Himself* persecuted as often as His disciple is hurt; He weeps with every disciple who weeps, He rejoices with every disciple who rejoices.

Jesus says that at the last judgment the wicked will hear the reproach, "*I* have been hungry, sick, or in prison and you did not visit *Me*". And He then explains that as often as one of

9

His little brethren suffered hardships, it was He Himself who passed through suffering.

The Lord Jesus is our leader in religion. But He might not pass an examination in grammar because He uses interchangeably the personal pronouns "he" and "I".

The Christian religion consists in becoming inebriated with love. Inebriated men confuse things and persons. The distinction between "I", "you", and "he" disappears. Therefore, when I speak, if I am inebriated with love for God, God speaks through me.

* *
*

Two thousand years ago Jesus said, "*I* am the Truth". And for 2,000 years this assertion of His has been falsified and quoted as meaning that Jesus said, "*He* is the truth". But He never said that *He* is the truth. He said, "*I* am the truth". If you make Him a "he", even with a capital H, you have lost the truth.

What can Jesus, the "he", the God embodied in a carpenter of 2,000 years ago in Palestine, tell you about modern techniques, about socialism, democracy, or military dictatorship, and which of these to prefer, about whether or not we should accept the philosophy of Teilhard de Chardin or the philosophical implications of Einstein's theory, about whether we should be fundamentalists or modernists?

What can Jesus, the man who lived 2,000 years ago in Palestine, tell you about the theory of evolution? Can He tell you to marry George rather than Steve? Can He guide you in any practical matter?

Jesus never wished to be "he". As a condition for His being the truth, He must always remain an "I". *I* am the truth, not *he* is the truth. If I wish to have the truth and to be the truth, Jesus must be for me an "I".

It is not true that He must *become* an I. He *is* an I. Luther says, "The Christian *is* Christ". This is the fact, though you may not realize it yet. When my eyes are opened, I say with St. Paul, "I live; yet not I, but Christ liveth in me". Then

I become sure of my own thoughts. *I* write a book, which means that God speaks through my book.

Men of God have always thought like this.

Luther wrote: "I have to distinguish between myself and my calling. I consider myself as the smallest. But my calling is untouchable . . . Nobody should have a high opinion of his own person, but everyone should mightily praise his calling to the glory of God. Even more. The man who holds the office has not even to prove what he says, he has to be listened to as God Himself".

*   *
*

To become a Christian means to become Christlike. In what sense? Not everybody is a Jew as Jesus was, not everybody a carpenter, not every disciple of His a male. In what sense then can I become like Him?

He lived a human life with the full assurance that He was right. In His time, like today, there existed hundreds of religions. In Galilee alone many nations and many religions met. He never chose any of these religions. He believed that man must choose *His.* Palestine was divided into many groups: the Zealots, the Herodians, the Essenes, etc. Jesus never chose among them. He spoke about earthly things, but others had to accept what *He* said. He never accepted what others said. He knew Himself to be the embodied truth. To be a Christian means to become Christlike, that is, a man without doubts about the message, a man who knows that Christ is not a "he". When this man speaks, Christ speaks.

Putting the realities of spiritual life in human words, I will have to use the personal pronouns, but my words will be transparent. Through them, you must grasp the reality behind them: It is the Lord who tells you "Come unto me". You have to come to *him* by seeing to it that he is no longer a "he" for you.

I have to make it very clear again. I do not call you to come to him. The sacred words are "Come to *Me*". Do not come to *him,* which means, do not have in the future

11

a "he" as an object of worship and do not be content with this.

The whole idea of subject and object is an illusion, which has been strengthened in us by linguistic structures. These will oblige me, too, to "misuse" pronouns. But I do so, conscious that what we call the "I" is only a temporary meeting point of different forces, which continually change their intensity and direction. Learn to think outside the categories of "I", "you", and "he". The thinker, the thought of, and the act of thinking are one.

There is one all-powerful "I". The ten commandments start with the words "I am God". Within this only God, we live and move and have our being (Acts 17:28). We form the inward life of God. We are not exterior to Him.

God continually contradicts the notion of an "I" of ours as opposed to His. Jeremiah does not wish to accept the call to become a prophet. He says to God, "I am a child"; but God answers, "Say not, I am a child . . . for I am with thee" (Jer. 1:6–8). Significant are the words of God, "Say not I . . . for *I* . . ." Where His "I" intervenes, the state of our "I" does not count.

Zacharias, when told by the angel that he would have a son, the future John the Baptist, says to the heavenly being, "I am an old man". This objection is cancelled with the words, "I am Gabriel" (Luke 1:18–19). For a man to speak in terms of an "I" when he hears a voice from heaven is senseless. It is again "not 'I', Zacharias, but 'I', the angel".

God calls a man "a fool" (Luke 12:16–20). This was the man who thought only about his earthly riches. It would have been easy to recognize him as a fool. In three verses of the Bible, he uses the words "I" and "my" nine times, not knowing that this "I" was meant to die on that very night and the "my" to pass into the possession of others.

We will come back to this idea later on. To come to God is just another way of saying to come to yourself, to your real being, to the One whose image and likeness you bear, to the only real "I".

12

Jesus told St. Catherine of Siena: "I am He who is, you are she who is not".

* *
*

In my church in Bucharest, I had a Russian member who did not know one word of Romanian, the language in which all services were conducted. He was never absent from church. During the sermon, he would read his Russian New Testament.

I felt a responsibility to him. I called him one day and said, "Look, I am your pastor. I would like to know what you understand from this book. Choose a part of it at your convenience and explain it to me!"

He read to me Chapter 1 of the first epistle to the Corinthians and then interpreted, "The apostle writes that Paul had planted the gospel and a certain Apollo had watered, but God gave the increase. From this he draws the conclusion that neither Paul, nor Apollo are anything, but only God. Now, if St. Paul and Apollo are called just nothings, how much is your worth, Brother Wurmbrand? God has called the things which are not. Be happy to be just a nothing".

I embraced and congratulated him for understanding the Bible better than I.

* *
*

Jesus says, "Come unto Me". Accept the call! Do not be one of the ice-cold hearts which very often are as hard and as unfeeling as the stones of the prison floor on which Jesus might have slept, after being arrested in the garden of Gethsemane.

* *
*

Jesus says, "Come unto Me!" and not only to pompous Church services. The great inquisitor in Dostoievsky's *The Brothers Karamasov* said to the Lord, "We have improved upon your work". Jesus in His humility is thankful for improvements. He has promised us that we will do even

13

greater works than He did. But He wishes you to come to *Him,* to Him alone.

Christianity has changed many times during the centuries. Christianity in the time of Jesus was different from that of the first Christian community in Jerusalem, which in turn differed from the first Christian churches in the gentile world. The state church after Constantine the Great was something else again. The church then changed in the Middle Ages, the Reformation, the time of rationalism, and the times of pietism, modernism, state-controlled and underground churches in Communist lands, and the charismatic movement in the free world. Origen considers Christianity as part of a divine movement which prepares for something even higher. Superior forms of Christianity may yet arise. All of them are vehicles of the one Christ, who never changes. He says, "Come to Me!"

*   *

*

How should I come to Him? In Luke 24:5, it is written that Jesus parted from his disciples. This parting is a definite and abiding fact, a truth valid for all our earthly life, except that the contrary of truth need not be an error. It can be an opposite truth. Everything in the world has a dual nature: so also the relationship between men and Christ. The fact is that Jesus parted from men; the fact is that Jesus can become an "I" in men.

Do you seek Jesus? Then the first condition for reaching Him is to fulfil what Jesus told the Roman soldiers: "If therefore ye seek me, let these (My disciples) go their way" (John 18:8).

Jesus has parted from them.

When the high priest asked Jesus about His doctrine, Jesus answered him, "Why askest thou me? ask them which heard me, what I have said unto them" (John 18:21).

Luckily enough, the discussion was interrupted by a slap which Jesus received from an officer who stood near by.

Otherwise, He would have received a terrible blow from the

high priest himself, who could have answered Him, "Whom among those who heard you could I ask about your doctrine? One of them sold you to us, and you will understand that he did it with many bad words about you. Another disciple of yours is just now in the court and says that you are only a man, a man whom he has never known. Your other disciples have fled. Men who have heard you are in the other room waiting to testify, 'This fellow said, "I am able to destroy the temple of God and to build it in three days" '—surely not a very attractive point of doctrine. You have spoken to thousands. They understood nothing. They will shout tomorrow, 'Crucify Him!' John, your beloved, is here but is silent. You are the only one who can tell us your doctrine. If you refuse, we will do without it".

The situation has not changed much since.

If you wish to know the doctrine of Jesus, let His disciples go.

The first recommendation I give to you is this: "Let everybody in the world go his way; let churches and those who repudiate them go their way, right or wrong; and you, answering only for your own soul, come to Jesus! Look neither to the right nor to the left, do not look behind, do not care about what others say! *You* come to Jesus!"

* *
*

Come so near to Him as to be one with Him!

When the first Christians met in the catacombs, they used in their sermons the following illustration:

A boy loved a girl to folly. One day he could not bear it any more. Late in the night, he knocked at the door of his sweetheart, asking her to allow him to enter. She asked him, "Who is it?" He answered, "It is I". Her reply was, "My chamber is narrow. There is room only for one. Go!"

He departed into the world to forget his sorrow. He could not understand her refusal, knowing that she loved him too very much. After years of erring around, he all at once had an illumination.

Late one night, he knocked again at the door of the girl. When asked, "Who is it?", he replied, "It is you." The door opened. His beloved embraced him and said, "I have waited for you a long time".

What dimensions has God? He speaks with Moses between the two staves of a box, in which the Jews carried the Ten Commandments given to them on Mount Sinai. Heaven is the narrowest place in the universe. It has place only for One. Only those will enter into heaven who have become one with Him.

Shakespeare says in "The Phoenix and the Turtle": "Number in love was slain". Love cannot coexist with multiplicity. Those who love are always one soul and one heart. Husband and wife are one. Christ and the Father are one. So is the faithful soul and Christ. In love, distinctions between a "he" and an "I" are impossible.

King Solomon says in his Song (Cant. 6:8–9), "There are three score queens, and four score concubines, and virgins without number. My dove, my undefiled is but one . . ."

*　　*

*

Before going further, let me repeat the warning: God speaks to you in the present book, setting before you a high responsibility. If you do not receive Jesus, you commit spiritual suicide.

There was a man who all his life had very great troubles. One night he tossed around in his bed, not finding rest. He asked God to show him what unseen enemy destroyed his life, and from behind a curtain this enemy appeared: himself! You are your greatest enemy if you do not receive Christ.

We are like the silkworm which prepares the cocoon in which it will develop. How do you build the house of your future?

In the Romanian town Lugoj, the director of the prison received an order to arrest the sub-director, a lieutenant. The director called the sub-director and told him, "Today we will have a new political prisoner. See to it that you prepare a cell for him!" The lieutenant took a warden with him and

16

chose the worst of cells. Now, all prison cells are bad, but some have a little more light, others less; some are damp, others are dry; in some you can take three steps to and fro, in others only two. He chose the worst of cells, the worst of straw mattresses. Then he came back to the director and told him, "I have prepared the cell".

The director said, "I would like to see it myself". He went to the cell with the lieutenant and asked him, "Do you not think that you should give the man better housing than that?" The lieutenant replied, "You are too softhearted, captain! That is the right cell for a bandit".

The director told him, "Well, you are the bandit. Please enter!" And the door was locked behind him.

We, all of us, decide our future habitation by receiving or refusing Christ.

* *
*

Those who refuse Him will have to suffer in hell.

It is a bad place; I know it. In spirit I dwell there often, because hell is not surrounded by the indifference but by the love of Christians. In Luke 16, it is written that some who are in heaven love those in hell so much that they would be ready to pass from heaven to hell only to be able to help. But they cannot.

Hell is a terrible thing. How awful to be there for all eternity with the devils!

St. Catherine of Siena once saw a devil and wrote that rather than look again for an instant on such a monster, she would prefer to walk until the end of her life on a bed of red coals.

And the devils will torment infidels. St. Anselm said, "In hell, souls are so utterly bound that they are not even able to remove from their eye a worm that gnaws it".

You had better receive Jesus!

Jesus speaks about a last judgment. I will describe it to you.

God will sit on a white throne, behind Him a curtain, before Him in one line those who have to be judged. God will lift

17

B

His right hand, and at this sign beings of unspeakable splendour, radiant in all colours, will appear from behind the curtain and will stand before each of those to be judged. Then the wicked will ask God, "Who is this beautiful being before me?" And God will answer, "This is you as you would have become if you had believed in Jesus". Then, in despair over what they have lost, the wicked will flee to hell, unable to endure the picture of what they could have become.

You will never be you, the radiant being, made in God's image, if you do not come to Jesus.

*   *

*

God calls you through me.

There is someone else to call you. This is your real self. In a parable, Jesus tells the story of a prodigal son who prematurely took his inheritance from his father, went to a distant land, and squandered the money in loose living. Then a famine ravaged the land. Having no money left, he took a job tending swine. Starving, he would have liked to eat the husks thrown to the pigs, but "no man gave unto him". At the end of his tether, the prodigal son of the parable—so the Bible says—"came to himself" and decided to return to his father.

"He came to himself"—what an expression! Where had he been until then? Well, we say in English, "he was beside himself". He was outside himself. He had not exercised his own mind, he had not been guided by the best impulses of his own heart. Like an ape, he had followed the selfish ways of others. Like a parrot, he had repeated their stupidities. Most men would rather die than think for themselves. Once the prodigal son "came to himself", to his real self, he implicitly returned to the truth and to his father. In the parable, God is the father.

It is simply not true that you have lived without Jesus until now. It was only that your real "you", the beautiful being created after God's own image, has not been within you. You belong to Jesus. You have not known it until now. The Son of God has been within you and would have liked to reveal Himself to you, but you were in a distant land (Gal. 1:16). Through me your real personality speaks to you. Right now, I am your conscience, your real I. I love your soul more than you love it yourself. You are a hodge-podge of all kinds of prejudices and beliefs gathered from others. The actor plays "Hamlet" one day, and "Othello" the next, but he is neither the prince of Denmark nor the jealous moor. He is himself.

You have acted until now as an atheist, an agnostic, a revolutionary, a drug-user, a sex-abuser, a moneygrabber, a pleasure-seeker, a churchgoer, or any number of things. But all these are only roles you have played. Your real you has been waiting, waiting. It speaks to you now through me.

Luther, a great teacher of Christianity, made a distinction between direct faith and faith which knows itself as such. When someone asserts "I believe" or "I believe not", he expresses his opinion about what happens within him. His opinion about himself may be as wrong in this matter as he can be wrong in judging others. One man may consider himself healthy while cancer ravages his body. Another thinks himself ill, but his malady is in his imagination.

Your infidelity can also be in your imagination. You may not have what theologians call "fides reflecta", a faith conscious of its existence. But you can have "fides directa", a faith which simply exists. A baby exists without knowing that what it has is existence. But its loving mother knows about its existence and needs. Likewise, you do not know what happens within you because your real you is outside waiting. I am your "you". I am your conscience.

As you read these lines you will find how right Plato was when he said that "knowing is recognizing". I will not tell you things which are new to you. You will recognize in my words the light which enlightened you when you came into the world. Later, like the prodigal son, you drifted far away from yourself. Now you are being called back. When you return, your faith will become conscious. The Son of God will be able to reveal Himself within you. Your coming to yourself will be identical with your coming to Christ.

*   *
*

You are reluctant? You say that religion is irrelevant? I fully agree with you. The question is only how relevant relevancy is. How relevant are you and I? How relevant is your or my opinion about what is relevant?

Walls determine the size of a room. Only the empty space between the walls makes the room useful. So does the empty space within the cup. We live on what is empty, not on what is full. For walking, are only the soles relevant? The whole foot walks. But the foot could not walk without those things which seem irrelevant to walking, like the heart, the lungs, the cortex, the spine, the law of gravity, the atomical and chemical structure of the earth, and the way itself.

Yes, religion is irrelevant. You can live without it, but you can also live without art, without books, without literacy, without trousers, without fresh air, without sunshine, without loving and being loved. But such an existence does not deserve the name "life". It is the "irrelevant" things which make life beautiful and rich in meaning.

You ask yourself what Jesus can give you. Why must someone be useful to you in order to be your love? Why this constant search only after what is relevant? Men followed Jesus long ago, when He predicted only His death on the cross and His own resurrection, long before He promised eternal life also to others.

Mary Magdalene loved Him and washed His feet with her tears, having no idea that she could obtain from Him forgiveness of sins and a place in paradise. She loved Him just for love's sake. Do the same!

*   *
*

Arise! Do not stop at the beggarly things which are "relevant!"

Life has changed more in the last fifty years than in the

20

5,000 before. Some are interested in quasars and novas and the expansion of our universe, others in mesons and quarks, others in genes. Do not busy yourself only with trivia, with things which minister only to creature comforts. Seek the ultimate reality. Seek the explanation of the whole. Seek God!

If you do, a thousand questions may arise in your mind, questions a true Christian teacher may ignore. The teacher from God does not teach what the pupil chooses but what the teacher considers good for him to learn. In spiritual things one does not need the answer to innumerable religious problems but rather what Jesus calls "poverty in spirit". The soul must become calm as the sea, which mirrors the beauties above.

The proper teacher does not answer questions. Neither am I prepared to give you complicated replies to your multitudinous queries. The best thing for a teacher of religion to do is to efface himself, to withdraw into the shadows, not to be the embodiment of a word of God, but only a voice through which the Master might say whatever word He wishes, or a silent lute awaiting His desires.

When Alexander the Great asked the philosopher Diogenes, "What can I do for you?" Diogenes answered, "Get out of the sun". This is what souls thirsty for God should say to theologians. The purpose of the present book is not to speak to you about Jesus, but to allow Jesus to appear Himself. He who became incarnate within an unknown stable, who became enshrined in the written Word, now humbles Himself even further. He uses the voice of a sinner to make you attentive to the whisper of your own inner voice, which is the voice of your conscience.

*   *

*

There are men who tell you, "Fight capitalism", or "Fight Communism", or "Fight Islam". Suppose one of these fights succeeds, what will be the difference? Nazism was fought against victoriously. Has the world become any better since? There are men who tell you, "Do not fight either capitalism, or Communism, or Islam. Make peace with them". What kind of peace can there be between those who hate each other? Peace is not the absence of war but the presence of love. There are men who tell you, "Do not care about fighting or making peace with capitalism, Communism, or Islam". If I care about none of the great problems of humanity, what have I a mind for? I say, leave them all! Seek God! He is all you need. When you have Him, you have the answer to all problems, because the problems will not be problems for you any more. Jesus says, "I am the life". This applies to you, too. You will simply live your life with Jesus at the controls, and this will be His life.

The eroding doubt will disappear. Jesus once asked one of his disciples, "Why did you doubt?" Peter had walked on the water and had been in danger of drowning. The disciple never answered the Saviour's question, neither did the latter insist. If He had, Peter could have answered, "I doubted that I would be saved from this deadly danger, because you are incalculable. So many of those who believe in God drown. Sometimes they escape in a miraculous manner. But you never know how it will be in your case". Peter would still have been wrong to doubt. This because, once you belong to Jesus, life and death are the same to you. He is eternal. So are you, because the distinction between "he" and "you" does not exist. Grammar has no place in real religion.

*　　*

*

Our adversaries say that religion is a kind of opium, an illusion. Well, is every illusion wrong? The man who drowns has the illusion of sleeping on soft cushions, the man who freezes, of resting near a heated oven. Some illusions are mechanisms of defence that help us pass over difficult moments. There exist good and bad illusions, as there exist good and bad thoughts. An illusion can be a loving mother who passes her breasts through iron bars and gives her imprisoned and dismayed child to suck. Illusions are a tremendous force. They can give new life and strength to those who are almost lost.

But the comfort of Christ is no illusion. It is reality.

You will ask how I know this. Christians believe that Buddhists and Hindus, and Jews, and Moslems, and atheists, and agnostics are all mistaken. They consider others to be taken in by myths. But what can happen to others can happen to Christians, too. They should check on their own beliefs, lest they be beguiled by myths.

An evangelist once told a Jewish boy of twelve that Jesus was the Son of God and that he would be lost if he did not believe on Him. Very earnestly 'the boy answered: "Pastor, the contrary also holds true. If Jesus is not the Son of God, and you believe on Him, *you* are lost". We must know that everyone, whether Hindu, or Jew, or atheist, or Mormon, or Catholic, or Protestant, rests his eternal life on what he believes; and nobody can simply dismiss the question of whether or not Christ is a myth.

Kant rendered mankind a great service. He showed, as nobody had before, to what extent the world is manufactured by the mind. We catch impressions through our senses; the impressions are categorized by our minds according to causality, finality, quality, quantity, modality. Out of this we construct a universe, our inner universe, through intricate operations of the mind. Then we speculate about these notions and make them more and more abstract. Our notion of Godhead is surely also the manufacture of our mind.

How far does it correspond to reality?

The possibility of deception is enormous. The adherents of all religions believe that the majority of mankind is deceived, because everyone believes that only his religion, or his lack of religion, is the truth. So, if the majority of mankind is deceived, this possibility exists for me, too.

Within the framework of religion, assuming the existence of God is already accepted, there still exists the possibility of deception. The Pharisees of old were sure that through their teachings they opened to men the gates of the Kingdom of Heaven. Then came Jesus proclaiming that their teaching closed the gates of the Kingdom. The Pharisees allowed

23

themselves to be slaughtered for their faith. Jesus died, asserting *His* belief.

Which of the two is true?

Dante says in his *Divina Comedia*: "Midway upon the journey of my life, I found myself in a dark wood, where the right way was lost". This is the experience of all thinking men.

We have one sure truth, and that is the quest for truth in the minds of men. A sure truth is that there exists in mankind an incessant search for the true, that mankind takes enormous pains to sift the true from the false, and this sometimes in a completely disinterested manner.

Why should we trouble ourselves to learn whether the sun goes around the earth or the earth around the sun? A knowledge of the truth about this makes not one penny's worth of difference to any one of us. Notwithstanding, we all pursue such incessant quests, impelled by an instinct which tells us that truth is desirable and should be followed.

In this quest we meet Jesus.

He does not make excessive claims.

He does not teach us to consider the founders of other religions as being His competitors or His enemies. In Solomon's Song (1.7) the other religious bodies are called flocks of the companions—not the rivals—of Jesus.

He does not speak about Himself as being only the truth. There exists one sentence in the Gospel of John (14.6) in which everything depends on punctuation.

What is the correct punctuation of Jesus' words, "I am the way the truth and the life"? I would say, "I am the way: the truth and the life."

Bottles of medicine are mostly mixtures. Jesus Himself says that in His teaching He gives us a mixture. He had in mind the circumstances of the way which everyone of us has to follow, the answer to the quests of truth, and the necessities of life.

Life based on truth alone would be impossible. How could we live calling every hunchback a hunchback and every ugly girl ugly? Life is basically unfair, endowing men so differently and burdening the majority of us with undeserved handicaps. We must say the truth without crushing life.

*   *
*

A boy was given two dimes: one for Sunday school, one for candies. He stumbled, and the coins rolled away. One he recovered, the other fell into the gutter. He said, "Well, Lord, there goes your dime".

Truth declares: one coin for candies, one for the Lord. Life always loses the coin reserved for holy purposes. Then truth condescends: "Would you not give at least one penny of the remaining coin or at least a sincere regret that nothing has been left for God?"

Jesus dwelt among us "full of grace *and* truth" (John 1 : 14). Which is more important, "grace" or truth"? The most important word is "and", the sign that we have a combination. Then the order of the two. Grace comes first. "And of His fulness have all we received, and grace for grace" (John 1 : 16). As to our receiving truth, the Lord has to wait longer. He is patient. He knows that nobody on earth can walk a straight line, the earth being a sphere.

*   *
*

There is in everyone a quest for truth and also a rebellion against its demands, and a doubting of the truth when it is discovered. Jesus is the only founder of religion who proclaims Himself to be the truth, and even more, the Son of God; and at the same time is an embodiment of doubt as to His own calling. He cries on the cross, "My God, My God, why hast Thou forsaken Me?" He is the synthesis between truth and doubt of the truth, and therefore He is the truth.

If Jesus had been an invention, the ones who invented Him would never have written in their gospels that they themselves had doubts about Him. They would never have said that they doubted Him, even after His resurrection. The Gospel is the only religious book of the world which expresses the truth

25

together with doubts about this same truth. Therefore, it is truth.

In Jesus, we meet God, a God who became specific, born in the fifteenth year of the reign of Caesar Augustus. He is not questionable, but He questions Himself and He is questioned even after His resurrection by His apostles. Therefore He is the truth on whom we can rely.

Yea, more. There is no believer to whom blasphemous thoughts do not occasionally occur, thoughts of quarrelling with God. Religious men repress these thoughts, which are part of their being. Thus they incapacitate their mind for the full truth. (Temptations should be brought to the bar of reason.)

The Bible is the only holy book of the world which propagates the loftiest ideas about God, at the same time saying scandalous things about Him; for instance, that He shall put a bridle in the jaws of a people—His creation—and will cause them to err (Isaiah 30:28), or that He is a slave trader (Joel 3:8).

In Ezekiel 6:12, God describes Himself as sending upon His chosen people famine and pestilences and blood and the sword.

God's prophet Jeremiah says to Him, "O God, thou hast deceived me; will thou be indeed to me as a deceitful brook and as waters that fail?"

The Bible praises God and expresses at the same time the harshest criticism which can be brought by the human mind against Him. By this we know it to be the truth. Then it dissolves these contradictions in a superior harmony.

*　　　*

*

Many say: "I already have a religion. Is not one as good as another? Why must I become a Christian?"

It is because Christianity contains the truth.

All religions are not alike. To put them on the same level would be like saying, "I like music so much that I do not care what kind of music it is, Beethoven or the Beatles". Religious people have to make a difference between the right religion and the wrong.

26

Christianity is the right religion because it comprehends in its all-embracing love, all other religions, and even the irreligious. It is the only religion in whose holy book it is written that we should not believe only "Christianity". The essence of Christianity is love, and *love believes everything,* not only Christianity (I Cor. 13 : 7).

It is the only religion which tells us not to restrict ourselves only to what this religion teaches, but to think on *whatsoever* things are honest, *whatsoever* things are just, *whatsoever* things are pure, *whatsoever* things are lovely, *whatsoever* things are of good report (Phil. 4 : 8), from whatever quarter these things come. And because it already embraces what is good and right from all quarters, it does not need to unite with any other religion.

It is *the* religion.

* *

*

There are many partial truths. Jesus is *the* truth, the whole truth.

During His earthly life throngs of people followed Him. He promised them nothing except a cross. Some followed Him because He cured and gave bread. But reason cannot explain why so many should have followed Him unselfishly at least for a time. People normally follow only demagogues, who promise them heaven on earth but can never deliver. Jesus was beloved because the glory of divine beauty shone upon His face. Sinners followed Him because He was full of grace and truth. He said simply, "Come unto Me", and they came. He says to you, "Come unto Me". Simply, come!

* *

*

You might say, "But I am a man of science. I cannot believe in all kinds of miracles such as the virgin birth. I know that there are laws of nature and that they cannot be broken". They have not been broken in the case of Jesus. For a being like Him, the natural thing was to be born of a virgin. For a

27

being like Him, it was natural to do things which no other man could do.

But in any case, the virgin birth and other miraculous incidents of His life which you accept with difficulty are of secondary importance. If somebody unites or equates a higher truth with lesser truth, the more important suffers and ultimately dies because of this misalliance. Nobody has ever called you to come to the virgin birth. You are called to come to Jesus. Come!

But do not dismiss lightly the virgin birth. Boris Pasternak, the Nobel prize-winner brought up under Communism, wrote in *Doctor Zhivago,* "Christ's miraculous birth teaches us that life should consist of the unusual instead of the commonplace, the festive instead of the workaday".

*　　　*

*

We call you to Jesus not because He is good, but because for you He became sin. In this sense, Jesus is not above you, He is below you. In order to come to Him, you do not have the difficulty of climbing but the ease of descending.

How many sins have you committed in this life? Have you murdered a hundred men? Jesus has taken upon Himself the murder of millions. Have you committed ten robberies? Jesus has taken upon Himself thousands of robberies. How many adulteries have you committed? Jesus has taken upon Himself the sexual impurity of millions of men.

So with lies, and with all other sin.

He meets with a sinner, a Canaanite woman, and addresses her with an admiring "O!" In Matthew 8:10, it is written that when Jesus heard the words of a Roman centurion, He marvelled at him and paid him a compliment.

It is a great thing to be an adorer of Jesus. It is an even greater thing to be a man admired by Jesus. Jesus knew this centurion to be a sinner, but how many sins did He have? Jesus took upon Himself, as His own, many more sins than those of the centurion.

In the Song of Solomon, there are the very words that the

heavenly Bridegroom, Jesus, says to His Bride: "I will *go up* to the palm tree" (Cant. 7:8). His approach to us is an ascension. Our approach to Him is one of condescension to the greatest sinner who has ever existed. There has never been a greater murderer, thief, robber, or liar than Jesus Christ—only not in the sense that He committed these offences Himself, but that, in a more profound way, He took them upon Himself. They are *His*!

It is easy to come to Jesus.

*   *

*

Are there some features in Jesus' character and teaching, are there some flaws in His life, which you dislike? He also disliked them. He refused categorically the title "good teacher" replying that only one is good, and that is God. He did not please Himself (Rom. 15:3), which means that if you had asked Him, "What opinion do you have of yourself?", He would have answered, "A bad one". He appropriated to Himself the sins of all men of all times. He felt them as burdening Himself.

Even if you dislike some things in His earthly life, come to Jesus! He did the things you dislike, because He had taken upon Himself your sinfulness and mine.

I once had a vision.

Surprised, I saw myself descending into a very low valley. I had believed heaven to be above us. A beautiful female angel, who guided me lovingly, explained that because many could not reach heaven, which was originally very high, because not all could bear the cold of the northern peaks, the heavenly had descended below any lowness. However low I might be, it would always be lower. We can be in heaven not only in sublime moments, but also in moments of despair.

*   *

*

A poor farm woman brought her daughter to the capital so that she might earn money as a maid. From what she

29

could send home, they will be able to buy some land and cattle.

The girl was beautiful and clever. She learned quickly that in a big city a girl like her could earn much more by not working than by working. She succeeded in attracting rich lovers. Passing from one to another, she gathered jewels, cars, and furs, and indulged in a life of fun.

In her life of pleasure, she forgot about her old mother altogether. One day she remembered her painfully. Taking the train to her village, she arrived late at night. Approaching the gate of her mother's house, she discovered that it was wide open. She was surprised, because she knew it had always been locked with great care.

She passed through the yard and saw that the room in which her mother slept had the light on. When she was on the threshold, the mother called from inside, "Jean, is it you?"

"Yes, mother. But how is it that the gate is wide open so late at night?"

"My daughter, for ten years, ever since you left, the gate has never been locked."

"And how is it that there is light in your room so late?"

"My daughter, for ten years the light has never been off. The loving heart of a mother waited for you."

The heavenly Jerusalem is our mother. She waits for us.

* *

*

You are uneasy, "If I accept Jesus, I have to accept the Bible, too. And it has been proven to be full of many errors".

People who have never read the Bible in the original languages in which it was written maintain that it cannot contain errors. I can assure you that it is full of "errors". Grammatical errors abound in it. They are in almost every sentence. Luther knew it, and his answer was that God does not speak words of grammar, but true realities. Sun, moon, heaven, earth, you, and I—we are words of God, His poem, verses, and rhymes of His creation. Nature, reality appear in our mind as incoherent. The Bible is errorless just because it reflects this incoherence.

A very frequent grammatical error in the Hebrew Bible is, for instance, the fact that the substantive is in the singular and the verb is in the plural. The question is only, whose is the error? I believe that the grammar is at fault and not the Bible. In English it would be like writing "He do a thing" instead of "He does". Grammatically it is wrong because grammar is false. Grammar begins with the supposition that there can exist a unitary "he" who does. But every "he" is very complex, with many contradictory impulses. Every "he" is a multiplicity. Therefore, the verb applied to him has to be in the plural form. So it happens that the Bible is full of "errors" and is always right. The standards of right and wrong wherewith we measure the Bible may be wrong. The Bible contains "errors" only because our notion of what is an error is erroneous.

*   *

*

"But to receive Jesus means to pass your time uselessly praising God. By the way, what does He need our praises for? Why is He so jealous for His prestige?"

He does not need your praises. You have need to praise Him. He is the supreme good. If you do not praise Him, you will praise yourself or other inferior beings, and will thus bar the way of your advancement.

Pasteur should not have been humble. Men like him do well to assert themselves. The life of thousands is at stake in their being recognized. How much more, then, is God justified when He asks for praise.

*   *

*

I call you to Jesus, because He can make you a saint, and the world needs saints. It has had plenty of politicians whose decisions have cost the lives of untold millions in foolish world wars and revolutions. It has had plenty of men of science, who provided the rulers of nations with the accoutrements of war and now with ultimate weapons. It has had a multitude of missionaries of many religions, who have created the religious

31

confusion reigning in the world. It does not have saints enough. One more is needed. You should be this one.

Come to Jesus!

* *

*

Your relationship with Him will be complex. Some know Him only as their Saviour. That is like knowing someone only as one's dentist. Jesus is more than Saviour. He will be your Lord. He will be your child, as much as He was the virgin Mary's child. Jesus says these strange words, "Whosoever shall do the will of My Father which is in heaven, the same is . . . my mother" (Matt. 12:50). He will be your brother. He will be your bridegroom. (In Hebrew and in Greek, the languages of the Bible, the words for soul, "neshama" and "psyche", are female substantives.) Jesus is the son of Mary, the Son of man, the Son of David, the Son of God. Jesus never called His mother "mummy", but only "woman", because the word "mother" would have circumscribed His relationship toward her in too narrow a sphere. He was not only her Son, but also her Saviour.

So He will be very diverse in His relationship to you. But more, He will be yours in what He is in Himself, beyond all possible relationships which you can have toward a human being. You will have not only someone to save you, to instruct you, but you will have JESUS.

* *

*

You may have attended church during a holy communion service. If not, do it out of curiosity. You will hear a priest or a pastor pronouncing over a piece of bread the words, "Take and eat this; this is my body broken for you". He means the body of Jesus Christ. Then he imparts a cup of wine, saying, "This is my blood shed for you for the remission of sins".

And the believers eat and drink, expressing by this act how intimately they appropriate to themselves the personality of Christ.

Jesus says that He takes all the sins of the world—that is,

32

your sins too, all of them—upon Himself, that He bears their punishment and dies for them on the cross.

If you come to Jesus and become a Christian, you will have the right to partake of holy communion. The words of the pastor, "This is my blood given for you", will bring you the good news which remains always fresh, that every injustice done by you is undone, that all your wrong is set right and what has been crooked is straightened. You will be able to say, "I am justified", which means, "I am *just* as *if I had* never sinned". You are free from the past forever. You have no more consciousness of sin. Your wicked deeds have not been repaired, but erased; your wicked thoughts have been blotted out; your bad words have beeen cancelled.

The salvation of Christ is full and complete. He saves to the uttermost.

You have the choice of accepting this sacrifice which Christ made on your behalf or of bearing the responsibilities of your sins yourself. Do not take it lightly. God does not pay at the end of every week, but in the end He pays.

Think it over well. How will you answer for all your sins? Why not rather receive His salvation? You have only to believe in Him in order to be saved. You need not even ask Him for forgiveness for your sins.

*   *

*

An interesting part of the gospel is what is not written For instance, you will never find mention that anybody asked forgiveness from Jesus for anything. People looked in His face and saw forgiveness written there. Peter once said such wrong things that Jesus had to call him "Satan". On another occasion, the disciples quarrelled about who should have the highest place in the kingdom. When Jesus was most in need of comfort, His disciples slept; they forsook Him and fled. Peter denied Him with oaths. Yet it never seemed to occur to any of them to say to Jesus, "I am sorry for what has happened". Neither will you have to use such words. Come to Jesus, even if you have a heart too proud to

33

c

acknowledge that you have been mistaken. To forgive is His profession.

He saved Mary, His mother. Nothing was more natural. She was His flesh. But it is written about all Christians that they are "members of His body, of His flesh, and of His bones" (Eph. 5:30). If I am a Christian and He does not take me to heaven, He will be there with some bone and muscles missing in His body. Who can imagine that He will not rather save us?

Your sinfulness is not a hindrance to your salvation. On the contrary, it is just what impels Him to save you. He understands all. Therefore He forgives all. If you can, pray to Jesus as Mary Magdalene does in *Doctor Zhivago*, "Unbind my debt as I unbind my hair". If you cannot pray, just leave it and come to Jesus without prayer. He forgives. He knows what will be the result.

*   *

*

In times of old, there were two brothers: the older, a pious and good man, the younger a rascal. The older often entreated his younger brother to change his ways. He prayed for him. But all was in vain. The teenager slid into worse and worse sins until one night he rushed into the room of his brother with blood-stained clothes and cried, "Save me! The police pursue me. I have committed a crime". The other one understood the situation. There was not much time for thinking. He told the criminal, "Let us change clothes". They scarcely had done this when the police appeared and, obviously, arrested the older brother because he was wearing the bloodstained clothes. He did not defend himself in court but on the contrary said, "I bear the full responsibility for the crime".

The judges had no doubt about his guilt, as he had been dogged from the very spot of the crime and had been found with traces of blood on his garments. He was sentenced to death. When asked about his last desire, he answered, "It is only one: that my brother should receive at the very moment of my execution this letter which I have written to him".

Next day, the youngster received the letter and read: "At this moment I die for your sin, in your bloodstained clothes. I am happy to perform this sacrifice for you. And I am sure that henceforth, in the white garment which I left you, you will lead a pure and holy life".

The youngster was overtaken with remorse. He tried to stop the execution. It was too late. But as often as his former comrades in revelry tried to call him to new wicked deeds, he replied, "In the pure garment left to me by my brother, who died on my behalf, I can no longer commit the evil deeds of earlier times".

Jesus knows that this will be the result of His sacrifice in your heart, too. He will save you, however sinful you might be.

If Judas had come to Jesus instead of trying to settle his ugly past with his ugly accomplices, we might know him today as St. Judas.

As a rubber erases a mistake, so does Jesus erase sins.

*　　*

*

The angels were not disgusted by the sores on the corpse of the beggar called Lazarus. They carried him to Paradise. Jesus, who during His earthly life had not a place to lay His head, is not choosy. He gladly accepts your home and your heart as a place of rest. It is surely better than nothing.

You have sins and they are red like scarlet. If a source of light recedes from the observer, the spectral ray corresponding to this radiation will be red. Sins are called red in Scripture because they put a huge and ever-growing distance between you and God. But the white of purity is at your disposal. White is the plenitude of light. Jesus is the Light of the world. You can have Him.

Only thus can you become righteous. Everything else is cant.

*　　*

*

We consider ourselves as righteous without this light only because we do not know the law of God.

A Brahman once boasted of the fact that he had never destroyed any living being in his life. Then a missionary showed him a drop of water under a microscope. The Brahman was afraid when he saw that he had swallowed innumerable beings as often as he had drunk water. But he quickly found a solution to ease his conscience. He destroyed the microscope. For the same reason, we set aside the Christian religion because it would show us our real state, that we are sinners.

When we realize that we are sinners, we abhor ourselves. We are disgusted at the state of our soul. Not so with God! The greatest pleasure for God is to exercise pity. Count von Zinzendorf wrote: "Nobody will have part of the mercy of God who has something of his own left, and something to show. Jesus is more thankful to men who give Him the opportunity to do something good for them, than when they attempt to do something good for Him. He prefers to see around Him men who need Him, instead of men who wish to do Him good. What should Jesus do for a righteous man? He seeks somebody in great need, and nobody is in bigger need than a sinner".

*   *

*

A prince once saw a tigress starving. Three cubs tried to suck her breast, but there was no milk. Now this prince was holy, and he pitied the beast. He knew self-sacrifice to be the highest virtue. He lay down near the tigress and cut his arm so that the sight of blood might arouse her natural appetite. He was devoured by her. But the tigress survived, and so did her little ones.

It is an insult to tigers to compare them with men. Tigers do not eat their own. Men kill their kin, even when they are not cannibals. Hitler killed millions of men. And he was a vegetarian.

Men had killed, had practised all the refinements of cruelty

36

and sin. Now they were starving. Mankind lived on sin, and all sins had been committed already, save one : deicide. Men had betrayed one another, but they had never sold out a Son of God.

So Jesus lay down near the tigress. He came to mankind. He aroused their cruelty and hatred. In order to continue to live, they had to eat His body—as He Himself foretold—and drink His blood. The tigress devoured Jesus.

And behold, beastly mankind can live again! This led Michelangelos and Leonardos to enshrine the crime of the race in painting and sculpture; it led Beethoven and Bach to memorialize it in music; and mankind translated and printed this story of its deicide into 1,000 languages. Christian civilization has been built on this crime. Tigers live because of this crime—the Borgias, the Torquemadas, the non-excommunicated Catholic Hitlers of all centuries. This crime has allowed tigers to gather huge treasuries on which fat clergy live. But this crime was for some tigers the last. Horrified at what they had done, some tigers became tame. They became saviours of life instead of destroyers.

Perhaps you can understand from this what Jesus has done for us.

* * *

In Colossians 1 : 14, it is written that in Christ we have redemption through His blood, even the forgiveness of sins.

If you are a citizen of, for instance, the United States, you have the privilege of living in a free country and of sharing in the benefits of its social welfare. In like manner, whosoever is in Christ and who belongs to Him has certain privileges, among which are redemption and forgiveness of all sins. We need this redemption, because we are sinners.

Dostoievsky wrote, "Every one of us is guilty of everything before everyone".

In II Chronicles 15 : 17, Asa, king of Judah, is reproached because places of idolatrous worship were not taken away out of another country, Israel.

Worthwhile social or religious institutions in your country can, by their example, have a good influence on like institutions in another country. Similarly, too, you are responsible for what is happening elsewhere. You need salvation, and you can have it through Jesus.

* *

*

Jesus can save because He gave His life to make you righteous.

The Japanese philosopher Ekken writes, "If a man will not give his life for righteousness, he does not know the relative value of righteousness and life".

* *

*

Jesus can save because He is the God-Man. Just as some chemical elements can combine only with certain other elements, not with all of them, so man is the only being who is compatible with God. God could not become animal or devil or vegetable or mineral.

Only a God-Man was possible, because we are of the same order; that is, we both have personality. Therefore, between man and God there is no possibility of distinguishing between the "I" and the "he". It is possible to distinguish God and man from animals or things. You can graft a fruit only on a fruit tree. You could never graft vegetables on a fruit tree. You could couple different breeds of sheep and get a hybrid. You cannot couple a rhinoceros and an insect. The fact that God could become man reflects the uniqueness of man. An unknown Greek poet quoted in the Bible (Acts 17 : 28) said rightly that we are God's offspring.

God could become only man. Men's sin attracted Him. He took it upon Himself. He gave His blood for our sins, and so He saved us.

* *

*

You are a sinner. You are not guilty of this.

I may be born ugly or misshapen or with a low I.Q. This

can be a terrible burden on me, which I have to face and deal with, though I have no guilt in my estate.

I was born a sinner. My parents and all my forefathers were sinners. It was not my choice. The Hebrew word for "sin" means "to miss the mark". We all fall short of the glory which would be ours without the innate sinfulness. It is there without my personal guilt.

The Old Testament tells the story of how Joseph, a Jew who had become ruler of Egypt, arraigned his brother Benjamin because in his sack had been found Joseph's silver cup. This cup had really been found in Benjamin's sack. But it is also true that Joseph had ordered his slaves to hide it there without the knowledge of Benjamin or of his many brothers. The purpose of Joseph in so doing was to develop a sentiment of solidarity in his brothers, who had shown themselves in times past to be very selfish men, even going so far as to sell their brother as a slave. Joseph wished to see if they would abandon Benjamin to his fate of suffering innocently as a thief or if they would stand behind him in his extremity. Fortunately, they stood the test of loyalty, and they were able to return to their father with great honour and an abundance of gifts.

Sin is a fact of life. It is due to some ancient happenings in which you had no personal part. It is a tragedy in which we all are involved and which is too deep to delve into. It is a tragedy somehow similar to being deformed or liable to so many painful and deadly sicknesses. We do not shrug the shoulder about being in the hospital, saying, "I have not created the virus". We fight it. A sickness may have its spiritual significance and value for us. Our sinfulness has its meaning in the universe. It makes us one with all other sinners. All mutual judgment disappears.

Dostoievsky tells the story of an angel who had no peace in heaven because of the torments through which the inhabitants of hell passed. Again and again he would descend to them asking them to remember at least some good deed which he then would bring before God as a plea to obtain their

39

release. But these had done no good deeds. In the end, a lady remembered, "I gave an onion to a beggar. Is this not a good deed?"

"It surely is," replied the angel. He flew to the archives of heaven and found in her file a note about the onion. He then took an onion to hell and told her, "Hold it with your hand. I also will hold it at the other end, and we will fly upwards. Thus you will arrive in heaven". They did so. The onion held well. The weight of the woman's body did not break it. She flew upward. When the others in hell saw this, they took hold of her garments, arms, feet. Others took hold of the feet of those who clung to the woman. Multitudes clustered beneath her, and the onion resisted. They all began to fly toward heaven. But the woman, looking down, saw them all and was afraid that the skin would be torn and she would fall. So she pushed the others away with her elbows, telling them, "Remain in hell, you sinners, who have never done anything good". In that moment, the onion broke. A sinner herself, she had judged others. This was the end of all her hopes. Because we are all sinners, we should love one another and not judge.

Do not seek the cause of your innate sinfulness! It is told in the story of Adam and Eve. Accept the fact that you are a sinner. There is a purpose in your sinfulness. And there is the possibility of being saved from sin. Jesus offers salvation. Get rid of the most deadly sickness of the world : sin!

President Coolidge of the United States was a man of few words. When he returned from church one Sunday, his wife asked him, "What did the pastor preach about?" He answered, "About sin." She asked again, "And what did he say?" Coolridge replied, "He's against it."

* *

*

Jesus loves His whole creation. I learn this from His disciples. St. Isaac prayed every day for the whole creation. So do I. Jesus must be at least as good as I am. Nobody is excluded from His love.

Now, in this creation, there is the human race, to which a

great catastrophe has happened. The race has fallen into sin. The life of every one of us has been marred by it. No one has quite escaped the stain of sin upon his name.

The remembrance of past sins makes us torment ourselves and others. There are today countless trouble-makers in the world. Nobody is a trouble-maker unless he is troubled himself. What troubles him are deeply rooted complexes, which very often are the result of past sins.

Now, how can sin be dealt with?

In times past, people would put their hands upon an animal so that atonement might be made for their sins. With some people, the ritual sacrifice was not an animal but another man, usually a slave. Such ritual murders exist even today among primitive peoples.

The Bible tells us in Hebrews 10:6 that God has no pleasure in burnt offerings and sacrifices. Our past sins should not be allowed to torment anybody in the world. They should not torment our fellowmen. Neither should we torment ourselves with endless remorses. Past sins must not be a motive for you to fill the pockets of clergy in order to receive absolution. Sin must not be a motive for squandering energy. Quietly accept the fact that we are sinners!

We have not become sinners by sinning. You sinned because you were a sinner. You will not become a thief by stealing. You steal because you *are* a thief. Sinfulness is your very nature, as it is the nature of every man. Except for Jesus, nobody who has ever lived on earth in human form has been anything other than a sinner. You must accept the fact that you have a nose, and hair, and lungs. These are part of being human. Accept also the fact that you are a sinner! Sin is part of being human.

Even saints sin. The apostles were sinners. Jesus told them in Mark 13:3 that Jerusalem and the Jewish state would be so utterly destroyed that stone would not remain upon stone. They did not pray for its preservation. They were not moved by the impending tragedy. They wished just to satisfy their curiosity *when* this would happen, although the happening had to mean death and slavery to millions of innocent people. They reacted to the words of Jesus like sinners.

As long as we dwell on earth, we will always have sins, as we will always have noses. They belong to human nature. But we can come to the point of having "no more conscience of sin" (Heb. 10:2).

The lives of many of us are like a car which has lights only in the back, so that the driver can see through the rearview mirror how many chickens or dogs he has killed in his driving. The lights should be in the front to prevent one from killing people! There is the possibility of leading a life which is not burdened by yesterday's sins. We should be careful not to neglect today's duties or make wrong plans for the future.

The past is erased by the fact that Jesus gave for our salvation His blood, about which Justin the Martyr writes that "it was not of human seed, but from divine power". Christ's blood was different from ours in that it could cleanse from sin.

Jesus purposely used the psychological mechanism of transfer, one of the powerful drives of the human soul.

It is part of sinful human nature to seek a scapegoat for everything that goes wrong. If you have mislaid something in your house and cannot find it, you feel better if you can blame your wife or your child. You still miss the object, but you feel relieved by the presumption that somebody else is the culprit.

A child hurts himself on a stool or table. If the mother beats the bad stool which has hurt the child, the child does not feel any more pain and begins to laugh.

Unscrupulous politicians often use this mechanism of transfer, putting the whole blame for everything wrong in the world on the Jews, the Blacks, the Whites, the Communists, the bourgeoisie, the king, the opposition party.

"American imperialists" are the scapegoats for the poverty of the world. But American imperialism is only sixty years old! There was poverty long before its rise, there was poverty before the very discovery of America, there was poverty before the first capitalist made his appearance, there was poverty under feudalism, under slavery and under primitive Communism. There is poverty under socialism, but we all need scapegoats!

Now, Jesus has also used this mechanism of transfer, which is so often misused, but in a good sense. Men seek a scapegoat, but there is something in man which makes him realize at least in part that his own convictions about the guilt of his scapegoats is illogical. Anti-Semitism existed before Hitler, tyranny before the Bolsheviks. One person or one institution cannot be blamed for social problems as old as humanity. But men need a scapegoat.

Therefore, God the Creator became man, and He tells us, "I take the full responsibility for everything that happens in My creation. I knew when I created man that man would fall into sin, but notwithstanding I created him. So I take upon Myself the responsibility for your sins, too. Instead of seeking other scapegoats, put all your sins upon me! I will gladly expiate them. I will bear the punishment of your sins". This satisfies the human mind. Now we have found the real Lamb, on which the sins of the whole world can be placed. He dies for our sins, and we no longer bear a guilty conscience.

We have in heaven a powerful intercessor with the Father who has been tempted in all things like us.

I happened to be a prisoner for a long period of time in a Communist country. I had as fellow prisoners a multitude of former judges and prosecutors, sentenced because they had, at one time, tried Communists. When these judges and prosecutors who had formerly administered the law were themselves forced to endure the hardships of prison life, they all said that if they were ever judges again, they would never hand down the harsh sentences they had given before. They had never realized before that five years of prison written as a sentence on a sheet of paper is not the same as five years spent behind bars. Nobody spends five years in prison. You make every day of prison separately, and each minute of each day is a pain apart. The experience of suffering changes a man's outlook on the question of punishment.

43

The incarnation of Jesus Christ and His death on the cross not only offered salvation to all who should believe on Him, but also enriched the Godhead! Therefore, it is written in Solomon's Song, Chapter 3 : 11, "Go forth, O ye daughters of Zion and behold king Solomon with the crown, wherewith his mother crowned him in the day of his espousals". Solomon is here a type of Jesus Christ.

From eternity Jesus Christ has had many crowns, but the most beautiful was given to Him by his blessed mother, Mary, when He, as God, espoused human nature. God had always judged men righteously, but He had judged them from the divine perspective. But when God became man, He saw human life from a human perspective. He knew by experience what it meant to be a poor child belonging to a despised race, to be hungry, to have nowhere to lay His head, to be tempted by woman, to be scourged, to be unjustly sentenced. God has been enriched through the experience of Jesus Christ. Not only does He save, but—as it is written in the Greek of Colossians 2:1 − "he graces our offences". God adds to our offences the grace of His own experience of human life. He has full understanding of our offences and forgives them whole-heartedly.

*   *

*

When you visit Jerusalem, you find something which puzzles the average tourist, but which the spiritual man would expect. There are two places considered to be the garden of Gethsemane where Jesus was arrested, there are several places of crucifixion, two tombs where He lay, and several places from which He is supposed to have ascended. This corresponds entirely to the fact that one gospel puts His crucifixion at the third hour, while another puts it at the sixth. According to one gospel, Judas the traitor participated in holy communion; according to another he was absent.

Historically, the sacrifice on Golgotha and the events connected with it happened just once. But this was the expression

44

of a liturgical, cosmic drama happening continually at different hours in different places under different circumstances, as the walls of Jericho, the cursed city, fell—archaeologists say—at various times during its history. Those belonging to the body of Christ have passed always and continue to pass through Gethsemanes, crucifixions and ascensions. Jesus suffered that you might be saved. This was a unique event. Christians suffer in persecutions that you might know about salvation, because it is the blood of the martyrs which is the seed of the church.

*   *
*

Behind Jesus and His suffering church is the Father who sacrifices His only Son for our salvation.

Is it right to sacrifice an innocent being for the salvation of sinners? According to our human standards—no! We would not consider a man righteous who, with power to prevent it, would nevertheless give his son to be scourged, spat upon, and crucified in order to save criminals from well-deserved punishment. God is righteous, but He has a righteousness apart, which we attribute to Him by faith. Only by doing so, only by considering righteous a God who, according to our standards, would not be so, can we apprehend that God considers as righteous sinners who, according to divine standards, would deserve only condemnation.

We cannot understand God's ways, but we know from His Word that He is prompted by love. Love frees us from sin. Love always frees. The word "free" comes from the old Etruscan word "freo", the Gothic "frion", which means "to love".

In Macedo-Romanian, they do not have the word, "to love". They use in its stead "to will". God not only loves you. He "wills" you with His all-powerful will. He wills to have you. All your resistance is in vain.

He loves you in the supreme sense of the word "love", which is to want somebody even if having him means death.

45

Therefore His love could not be expressed by any other means than a painful death, by way of Golgotha.

* *

*

On Golgotha, your debt toward God was paid. Your sins were expiated.

The greatest penitent does not desire to have his sins forgiven so much as God desires to forgive them. Proof of this is that none of us is so eager to give an hour for prayer or money for a Christian cause as God was eager to give His Son for our salvation.

* *

*

You are not like Jesus. You will continue to sin. But you will say about every sin of yours, "It is not mine; it belongs to Jesus, who will deal with it".

But will not the remembrance of past sins continue to trouble you?

I once told a mass-murderer the story of the two brothers, quoted above, in which the older gave his life for the younger, asking from him only one thing: to live henceforth, in the white garment which he had left him, an unspotted life. The murderer became a Christian. I asked him some time later if he was joyous at having been freed of his past through the sacrifice of Christ, our older Brother. His answer was, "I will be joyous only when an occasion arises in which I am able to play toward another sinner the role of the older brother and suffer for him". The occasion presented itself, and he became a happy man.

You can be happy even without such special occasions. Every man who becomes a Christian becomes an innocent sufferer because he bears punishment he no longer deserves. Immanuel Kant wrote, "The criminal has a right to punishment". A former murderer, liar, adulterer, drunkard, or sinner of whatever kind will continue to suffer the results of his past life even after his conversion. Through repentance he has become an entirely new creature who normally would not

46

have to suffer. The sorrows and pains which the new man suffers for the old man are a continuation of the sufferings of Christ. Do not worry: you will have your part of suffering and also the joy of being able to suffer.

But you will have been saved from all your sins.

*   *

*

Is a man who has been cleansed from all his sins still a man? The question is legitimate. He will not be a mere man any more but a child of God, a partaker of the divine nature.

Up to a certain stage, the embryo of a man cannot be distinguished from the embryo of an ape, which does not mean that the difference does not exist. The proof of its existence is that one embryo becomes a man, while the other becomes an animal. So those around you will not be able to distinguish easily between you, a child of God, and some good moral man. But there will be a tremendous difference. There might still be many sinful things in your life, but you are saved.

*   *

*

Good moral men who do not believe in Christ are also sinners, and their fate is to suffer the pangs of hell and eternal separation from God.

In English, the word "love" means very different things in the propositions "I love apple pie", "I love Mummy", and "I love God". So "eternal" may not mean the same thing when applied to heaven and to hell. But in any case, those without Christ will be lost and will have to suffer, whereas for you, a child of God, "dying" will mean entrance into a new, beautiful world. Death wears for us a mild face.

Do not worry about whether hell is eternal in the absolute sense of the word or whether it might end after a very long period of torment! It is an idle question.

If Jesus had said this much, that the punishment for sin will be to have boiling water poured just once over your whole naked body, would you commit the sin? One thing is sure from the revelation given by Jesus: it is that the punishment for sin will be worse than this.

*   *

*

We are saved by the grace of Christ. With our sins we pierced His heart, and from this pierced heart came blood which cleanses us from these sins.

The Bible records for use the seven words spoken by Jesus on the cross:

(1) A prayer: "Father, forgive them because they do not know what they do".

(2) A word to a thief crucified near Him: "Amen, amen I say unto you, Today you will be with me in paradise".

(3) A cry of despair: "My God, my God, why hast thou forsaken me?"

(4) A word to John about Mary: "Behold, your mother" and a word to her: "Behold, your son".

(5) An expression of need: "I thirst".

(6) A word of assurance: "It is fulfilled".

(7) A word of prayer again: "Father, into thy hands I surrender my spirit".

Through Christ's suffering on the cross we are saved.

But tradition records an eighth saying of the crucified Lord. Jesus, it is said, told the soldier who would soon pierce Him, "Friend, there is a shorter road to my heart than that".

*   *

*

Jesus saves not only from sin, but also from the solitude which oppresses so many. You will enter into close communion with Mary, the mother of the Lord, the saints of all ages, the angels, and more: you will walk continually in the companionship of the Lord Himself. You will also find loving brethren and sisters in the faith.

*   *

*

Jesus saves from the tyranny of the circumstances of life. The beautiful lotus flower grows out of mud and filth. It thrives in unattractive places. It blossoms where oppressive poverty reigns. It furnishes breathless purity in stinking yards. So will be your new life : full of glory even if it is poverty- and sorrow-ridden. You will live far above your environment. Out of misery, poverty and ,dirt, holiness will come.

You have been a slave of your surroundings. Now you will be free.

At an auction in Lexington in the United States, a beautiful slave, Elsa, was for sale. The young Methodist minister Fairbank competed with a Frenchman. When the Frenchman hesitated to raise the bid, the auctioneer pulled Elsa's dress back, showing her breasts : "Who is going to lose a chance like this?" Later, he lifted her skirts to bare her body : "Who is going to be the winner of this prize?" Fairbank got her and said, "I bought her to free her".

All kinds of political and religious movements wish to have you for their own pleasure and profit. Jesus desires nothing from you for His own good. He paid the biggest price—His own life—just out of love, to free you, for your good.

All honour to Pastor Fairbank. He served seventeen years in prison for anti-slavery activities. But who can put in words the honour due to Jesus, who died on the cross to set us free from the slavery of sin, death, and circumstances?

* *
*

There is no limit to our future growth. It is not only until death that you will grow in knowledge of God and virtues and inner beauty.

In a parable, Jesus teaches us to allow the children of His kingdom and the children of the wicked one to grow not until death, but until the end of the world (Matt. 13 :40). Christians will grow after death, too.

We have a very high aim. We wish to become like Christ.

What we are has been fixed by circumstances without our consent. Our real "I" is what we would like to be, if the ordering of things were in our hands. In our hours of religious meditation and contemplation, we dream about being a

49

Jesus in miniature. Fortunately, we have more than our short earthly life to reach this goal.

*　　　*
*

Jesus saves from anxiety. You know that God is love, and you do not have to worry.

With God on his side, one of the heroes of the Old Testament, Joshua, slew giants like Og and Sihon. You also will defeat huge forces gathered against you. Your quietness will give you the victory.

When my son Mihai was small, he once asked me, "Father, what should I do? I am bored". I replied, "Think about God!" He said, "Why should I with my little head think about the great God? Let Him, with his big head, think about me, the little child".

Christ is the head of the church. As long as there are no wrinkles on his brow, there is no reason for you to have wrinkles on yours.

If Jesus is the head, let Him think! The leg does not have to think, nor does the head have to walk. Therefore Jesus said, *"Take no thought how or what you shall speak"* (Matt. 10:19), and, *"In such an hour as ye think not,* the Son of man cometh" (Matt. 24:44).

For a Christian it is false even to think rightly. His mind is passive in order to receive impulses from Christ. It is never active on its own.

Luther sometimes went to the window in the evening and asked, "God, is it my world or yours? Is it my Church or yours? If it is your world and your church, take care of them! I go to bed. Good night, my God!"

You do not have to carry the whole burden of your life. God carries it.

*　　　*
*

Freedom from anxiety in the Christian life goes very deep. You do not have to worry even about your mistakes. In every mistake you make in life lies the seed of an equivalent benefit.

50

The Old Testament tells us about a lad, Joseph, who made the mistake of telling his brothers his dreams, which were offensive to them. This mistake resulted in Joseph's becoming ruler of Egypt. A Christian can have confidence even in his mistakes.

* *
*

Just as you are not to worry about this life, so you are not to worry about the next.

Once when Baalshem, founder of the Hassidic movement in Judaism, passed through a period of despondency and feared that he had lost eternal life, he comforted himself with the words, "If I love God, why do I need eternal life?" What is eternal life if it is not the knowledge of God and His Son Jesus Christ?

Therefore, all worry for tomorrow ceases. Your food will be manna, and manna has to be collected daily. You cannot treasure it up for the next day.

Jesus saves from the fever of ambition. Jesus Himself was never worried because He was known by so few. He lived so as to make Himself worthy to be known.

Jesus will teach you not to cherish inordinate ambitions that goad you on, nor to stretch yourself beyond your reach. As a Christian, you will accept yourself with your assets and liabilities. You will never attempt the impossible, but you will measure the height of the tower for which you have material.

* *
*

Jesus saves from complications in life. In Exodus 20:25, God commands, "Thou shalt make an altar of unhewn stone", that is, a very simple one. The enemy of simplicity is our sense organs with their separate and limited functions. Chuang Tsu said, "The eye is a menace to clear sight, the ear a menace to subtle hearing, the mind is a menace to wisdom, every organ of the senses is a menace to its own capacity. Sad it is indeed that men should look upon these seats of menace as their greatest treasure". Man's real treasure is the inward

51

vision, an over-all perception that can come into play only when the distinction between inside and outside, between self and things, between this and that has been entirely obliterated. This is the chaos, the *tohu-vabohu* as the earth was when God first created it. Every system of our mind is a falsification of the creation, which is not systematic. In science, Heisenberg finished with systematics, introducing the indeterminism factor. Things do not happen according to our systems.

Most men suffer from lopsidedness. Concentration on one segment of life prevents one from appreciating the whole gamut of human experience.

When you become a Christian, you become all-embracing.

Nietzsche wrote: "The wishing not to see what one sees and as one sees, is almost the first condition for all who are party in any sense. Every partyman becomes a liar. The eye sees according to points of view. Convictions are prisons. To be able to see, free of all convictions, is part of strength". Jesus is the truth beyond your convictions about what is true. He sets you free.

*　　　*
*

Men who do not belong to Jesus look at things from their own viewpoint. They do not know that every viewpoint is a point of blindness, because it incapacitates them for the understanding of every viewpoint which differs from theirs. From a certain viewpoint, a room has no entrance door. From another no window or no ceiling. You can know the room only by an intuition of the whole or by changing viewpoints.

Jesus saves you from viewpoints. Reality is not only material. It contains also spirit. So it knows itself. Jesus is the Logos, the self-knowledge of material and spiritual reality.

Jesus saves us from a limited horizon. Just as there exist sound waves beyond human perception, so there are light waves which we cannot see. We see only wave lengths between 3800 and 7600 Ångströms. Below 3800 are the ultraviolet, the X- and Gamma-waves; above 7600 are the micro- and radio-waves. Through instruments, we see many times as much reality as with the unaided eye. But there exist in addition farsightedness (the church elders are called in the Greek Bible "presbyters", far-seers), insight clear vision, the mystic vision, and above all, the beatific vision, the seeing of God face to face. Whoever does not have these is still more or less blind. We consider the eye the organ of sight, when in fact it prevents us from seeing the ultimate realities. Jesus saves us from the illusions of our senses.

The sun and the moon quarrelled once. The sun said, "The leaves on the trees are green", whereas the moon said, "They are silver". The moon said, "Men usually sleep", whereas the sun said, "They are usually in motion". "Why then is there such a silence on the earth?" the moon asked. "Who told you this?" the sun wondered. "There is much noise on earth."

So they debated. And then the wind appeared. He heard the talk and laughed. "What is this whole quarrel about? I blow when both the sun and the moon are in the firmament. During the day, when the sun shines, it is as the sun says. There is noise on earth, all men move, and the leaves are green. But during the night, when the moon shines, everything changes. Men sleep, silence reigns, and the leaves get a silver colour. When clouds cover the moon, the leaves even become black. Neither you, sun, nor you, moon, know the whole truth."

Jesus is master of sun, moon, wind, clouds. He sees reality as a whole. It is His understanding of the full truth which He imparts to His disciples.

He is the full truth because He is the only one in whom truth has never been distorted by sin. Every sinner is emotionally attached to something wrong, and this throws a shadow on the truth. Christ was sinless and knew Himself to be so. He was never hesitant or uncertain in dealing with others. He never questioned the wisdom of having been too severe. He never asked Himself if He should not have been gentler. His life was woven in one piece as was His garment. He came to each new duty untrammelled by accusing memories. Thus He was able to speak with authority. He was able to proclaim Himself as truth.

53

The church to which you will belong if you receive Christ is the continuation of His incarnation. You will walk through life with the same assurance He had.

* *

*

Without the full truth, your whole life will be a failure and, if you are a very gifted person, a catastrophe for others. The greatest mischief to mankind has been imposed by its geniuses, if they propagated with art and skill or enforced by dictatorial measures their limited viewpoints. How useful they could have been if they had renounced their own viewpoints for the truth as it is in Jesus.

* *

*

Jesus frees you from reason in matters of faith. Luther says, "Whosoever wants to be a Christian should tear the eyes out of his reason and not know anything of it, and even kill it as one who will not enter into the Kingdom of heaven". Christians sacrifice their intellect and so get rid of its unavoidable errors, when it interferes in a sphere where it cannot be effective.

* *

*

Seekers after truth must take heed to two warnings. One given by Tertullian : "Christ did not call Himself the custom but the truth". The multitude worship custom. The Christian will find himself with the minority or even alone. The second warning was given by Emerson, and it derives from the first : "God offers to every man the choice between truth and repose. You cannot have them both".

* *

*

Jesus saves from hatred.

It is remarkable that the Evangelists tell the story of Jesus' sufferings without one single bad word or epithet for those who inflicted the sufferings on Him. The only exception is Judas, who is called a traitor.

The apostles had no resentments, no grudges. Therefore there is restraint in the style of their writings.

You will be saved from hatred, too.

Why should you hate a man? If he does wrong things, it is because he does not know what he does. You who know the law of God will treat him with benevolence and justice.

*   *
*

Jesus is a very complex being. He has many aspects.

The Hebrew language does not have a word for "face" in the singular. It has only the plural "panim"—"faces". Every Hebrew word which ends in "-im" is plural. There is a deep meaning to this fact. The Hebrew language, in which the revelation of God has been given, does not acknowledge that a man has only one face. We all have many faces. Therefore, the labels "murderer", "thief", "crook", "saint", "Protestant", "Catholic", "reactionary", "revolutionist", are all false. Men cannot bear one label because they have many dimensions, and every one of us is an alloy.

Iron exists only as a concept in our mind. In nature, you will never find iron alone. You find it always allied with something else. The same is true of men. To approach or receive a man puts you already in a relationship with a very complex being. You might be very much attracted to his physical appearance, while his character might be repulsive. Highly intelligent people can be very wicked. One's relationship toward a man must be based on the different aspects of his mental, physical, and spiritual qualities.

This is all the more true in our relationship with Jesus.

To come to Jesus means to come to the saving Jesus, to the suffering Jesus, to the fighting Jesus, to the crowned Jesus, to the whole Jesus, and through Him to God.

*   *
*

It is really not easy to find God. We are before God as the judge before a defendant who refuses to testify. We must find God by means of presumptions.

55

It is very difficult to find a being defined by St. Augustine as a circle, which has its centre everywhere and its boundaries nowhere.

Modern technical knowledge and the miracle of television allow men to be everywhere, the centre of a circle with a very wide boundary. To a small degree this helps us understand a Being with no boundaries at all and a centre everywhere.

If God has His centre everywhere, I reckon myself to be the centre. I find Him then within myself.

I begin by trying to see God in what He has created. In Proverbs 20:12, it is written that Jehovah God is the one who made the hearing ear. It is enough to think about your ears, to come to a belief in God. The curves, hills and gullies of the ears allow us to determine from which direction sound is coming and the approximate distance of its source. Every convolution and crinkle helps in the perception of sounds and echoes. When you hear a sound above you, the tiny echo added by your ears' crinkles will differ from that added to a sound coming from below or behind, and so you will be able to discriminate. When you hear a sound coming from your right, then your right ear hears it just before your left ear does, and vice versa. Thus sounds are perceived.

If there were no God, how could you explain a flying machine or parachute as subtle and perfect as a dandelion?

The scientists in aerodynamics have calculated that it is impossible for the bumblebee to fly. But the bumblebee *does* fly, oblivious to the computations of aerodynamic specialists. Can you explain this, without a God?

If you do not see God, it does not mean that God does not exist. It might mean that you are blind. Now, blindness is not a positive attribute. It is just the absence of sight. Likewise, atheism is the absence of knowledge of the truth. You grope if you do not know God.

*   *

*

What is God like?

A man who had been blind from birth once asked someone

to give him a glass of milk and queried, "What does milk look like?" The other man answered, "Milk is a white liquid". The blind man asked, "But what do you mean by white?" The other man answered, "White is the colour of a swan". The blind man asked, "What is a swan?" The other replied, "A swan is a bird with a bent neck". The blind man asked again, "What does bent mean?" The other man said, "I will bend my elbow and you will touch it, and then you will know what bent means".

The blind man touched the bent elbow of the other man and said, "Now I know what milk looks like!"

In a book, even in the Bible, only words can be used to tell about God. These might seem ridiculous to you, as it seems ridiculous for a blind man to know the appearance of milk from a bent elbow. But we are all very limited and by nature blind to the all-comprehensive, omniscient, omnipotent God. We come to know Him by approximations. Read the words, forget about them, look at the ear, the dandelion, the bumble-bee, and simply believe that God is!

*   *

*

The English word "God", as well as the corresponding German and Scandinavian words, comes from the Sanskrit "Hathu", which means, "The one to whom sacrifice is brought". Who is worthier of sacrifice than God? In the form "Huta", the word means, "The one invoked". Whom else should we invoke than the Creator?

The word "Deity" comes from the Sanskrit "Deia", to shine. He shines as the sun and causes you to shine. Throw yourself trustingly in His arms!

Some beg for alms. Some bestow them. In the great game of life He, the Incomprehensible, encompasses all. He enjoys everything twice, because He is the Giver and the Receiver of every gift. By uniting with God through Christ, you will also know unspeakable joys.

*   *

*

A man came to a Christian and complained about a great sorrow. The Christian recited the creed: "I believe in one God, the Father almighty, Maker of heaven and earth, of all things visible and invisible". The man in pain answered, "It is enough. Now I am comforted".

Do not surmise that I speak to you about my God. I tell you about yours. He is the God of Abraham, Isaac, Jacob, Richard. He is your God, too. He can be your loving Father, and as such He causes all things, visible and invisible, to work together for your good.

What is He? The French have a saying, "Un Dieu défini est un Dieu fini". (A defined God is one with whom you have finished.) We do not know the structure of an atom and yet wish to explain a holy trinity!

Tolstoi, when asked, "What do you think about God?" replied, "What can an infusory think about man?"

We do not have to speculate about Him, but simply acknowledge Him in all our ways. A. Compton, Nobel Prize winner in physics, wrote, "The hypothesis that there exists an intelligent God gives a more plausible explanation for the universe than any other hypothesis". And Einstein, whose name the universe bears, wrote, "My religion consists in the deeply felt conviction about the existence of a higher Being, who reveals Himself in the world which we can comprehend".

If Einstein could believe in God, you can too. You are meant only to believe in Him, not to dissect Him.

A man can surely live without God, too. We all use inventions of scientists. We do not know the scientists personally. We Christians are men who have the passionate desire to know the inventions but also the Inventor of the universe.

*　　　*

*

When the shepherds came to see the little babe Jesus, they saw Him with Mary. Those who stood on Golgotha saw Jesus with Mary. Those who assembled in the first church assembled with Mary. Mary cannot be separated from her Son. We cannot adore Him without venerating her.

In human conflicts, people usually take opposite viewpoints. This is what happened during the Reformation. Some had exaggerated the role of Mary so much that others simply left her out of the plan of salvation.

It is said that a Protestant and a Catholic died at the same minute, and both went to heaven. The Catholic immediately bowed before Mary and kissed the hem of her garment. She caressed him on his head and said, "You have served me faithfully. May I introduce you now to my Son?" And then, for the first time, he made the acquaintance of Jesus Christ.

The Protestant, on arriving in heaven, immediately knelt down before Jesus and showed Him his respect. Then Jesus said to him, "May I introduce you to my mother? You seem not to have known her during your earthly life".

Jesus is a Person of the Godhead. He belongs to the triune God, to the Creator. Mary is only a creature, but she has her role in the economy of God.

In Psalm 22:9, the Messiah speaking through the prophet says, "Thou art he [the Lord] that took me out of the womb". It is the only part of Scripture where a man is referred to as having been taken out of the womb of a woman. Otherwise, both in the Old and the New Testaments, the expression is that he comes from the loins of his father.

Jesus is the One born of *the* woman ("Haishah" in Hebrew, prophesied in Genesis 3:15, the one woman with a special role in history, whose seed shall bruise the head of the serpent).

Jesus never called her mother. It would have been too common a name. He always called her "woman", hinting at the fact that she is this one woman foretold in Scripture, whose radiance cannot be put in words.

The Bible puts a question: "Who is she that looketh forth as the morning, fair as the moon, clear as the sun, and terrible as an army with banners?"

Finding the answer is not difficult.

She whose bridegroom became her babe is the beautiful one.

Every century she becomes more beautiful, yet sadder because of so many sufferings and betrayals.

* *
*

The Christian is Christ, His body, His flesh, His bone. If she is the mother of Christ, she is our mother, too. Jesus is the head, we are the body. The mother of the head is also the mother of the body. Luke calls Jesus her firstborn, because we are also her children.

When Mary sees you, she sees Jesus. No child is ever too dirty for a mother to wash, too bruised by any fall for her not to kiss away the hurt, too headstrong and selfish for her not to love.

God honoured Mary. Why should I not? She is near to every cross and to every altar, as she was near to Jesus on Calvary.

I wonder only that our Orthodox and Catholic friends do not take heed to the words of the Psalmist (71:16): "I will make mention to thy righteousness, even of thine *only*". Mary does not like it when attention is diverted from God to her, a humble servant.

I am also not at ease when she is called "mother of God". The council of Chalcedon had all the reason in the world to give her this title as against the Nestorians, who did not acknowledge the unity of the two natures of Jesus, the human and the divine, in one single person. But in everyday use, this title degrades God. If God has Mary as mother, He has St. Joseph as adoptive father. In the end, we have a God with a multitude of aunts and uncles and cousins.

So there are mistakes on both sides in the attitude taken toward Mary.

* *
*

There are some Christians who have as little pity for the suffering Jesus as those who tore His divine flesh with scourges. But there are others whose supreme joy it is to share his sufferings.

60

In Zechariah 11:1 it is written: "Open thy doors, O Lebanon, that the fire may devour thy cedars". Quite a demand! When you see a fire approaching, open your doors that it may burn down your possessions!

Knowing that our Lord has suffered for us, we Christians open the door to sufferings, even very severe ones. We open with gladness and receive sufferings as friends.

In II Peter 1:14, the apostle speaks about his impending crucifixion and says, I know "that shortly *I must put off* this tabernacle" (he means the tabernacle of his body).

Now, he did not put off his body; he did not commit suicide. He was crucified head-down by Roman soldiers. But St. Peter had so readily opened the door and agreed to his crucifixion, as foretold by Christ, that he considered it an act of his own. This is the Christian attitude toward suffering. We will it.

* * *

As Christians we are unruffled when bad words are spoken against us. We know that a wicked man who reproaches a Christian is like one who spits at heaven: the spittle does not soil heaven but comes back and defiles his own person. The slanderer flings dust upon another only to have the wind return it to himself. The virtuous man cannot be hurt by slander, and the misery another would inflict on him returns to the sender.

It makes no difference to the Christian whether he is praised or insulted.

A man asked St. Macarius, "What does it mean to die to the world?" The saint answered, "Go to the cemetery, stop before every grave, and say to the dead bad, insulting words". The man wondered at this command but did as he was told. Macarius sent him again, this time to stop before every grave and say flattering words to the dead. This he also did.

Macarius then asked, "Were the dead angry when you insulted them?" "No", was the answer. "Were they pleased when you complimented them?" The answer was again "No".

61

Macarius pointed out the intended lesson: "This then is what it means to die to the world".

We accept suffering under any false accusation. My wife, Sabina, adds at this point: "Suffering inflicted upon us by the will of God does not contradict love. It is one of its methods. Therefore Jesus calls God, who willed His crucifixion, *Father*".

St. Joan d'Arc was burnt as a witch, St. Thomas Moore was executed for treason. Likewise Bonnhoeffer. In Russia, some Christians are falsely accused of ritual murder, collaboration with the Nazis, theft, etc., and are given severe sentences.

*   *

*

Whoever becomes a Christian says with St. Peter, in Luke 22:33, "Lord, I am ready to go with thee, both into prison, and to death".

Every Christian goes to a sort of prison. It is written in the Song of Solomon that the Christian is a sealed fountain, a closed garden. It is as difficult to visit him as it is to see a prisoner. In the ark which saved him, Noah was shut up. The wise virgins were locked in the bridal room with their bridegroom. You cannot be His except behind a locked door.

Every Christian goes with Jesus to death. He dies to sin, he dies to the world, the flesh, and the devil.

*   *

*

I have seen suffering Christians dance for joy. Can you understand why?

There was once a fiddler who played so beautifully that everybody danced. A deaf man who could not hear the music considered them all mad. Those who are with Jesus in suffering hear this music to which other men are deaf. They dance and do not care if they are considered insane.

Other men could not understand the joy of the suffering Christians, just as a frog in a well could not understand the mighty ocean.

The Christian can rejoice even in the most unbelievable

circumstances. One of the possible translations of the Hebrew title of Psalm 4 is "Song of the one who rejoices when he is vanquished".

But there are many tears mingled with the joys of Christians.

The friends of Jesus suffered over the fact that He rode towards Jerusalem at the pace of the slowest animal, a donkey. He chose the pace Himself.

They tried at least to make His riding more pleasant. They put their coats on the donkey. Others put their coats on the road, in the path of the animal, so that the garments were torn and tangled in the feet of the donkey. The pace of Jesus was slowed down even more.

We suffer because peoples chose constantly to release Barabbas, a murderer, rather than the Messiah who came to save them. They do it even today.

*   *

*

Those who do not seek God in suffering men will not find Him. Meister Eckhart says: "You seek something through God, and you are like somebody who would make out of God a candle to use for its light. Once you have found what you sought, you throw away the candle. Some people would love God as they love their cattle. The cattle you love for their milk, and for the cheese, and for your own need". But those who love God for Himself, not only for His gifts, love Him also in suffering men.

How sorry we are for those who have adored Christ in the spirit, who have looked up to His divinity, who have bowed before the altar in His sanctuaries, and who do not recognize Him when He appears to them in the form of a sufferer.

When St. Joan d'Arc was in prison, no hand was lifted to help her. Charles VII, king of France (whom she had fought for), did not make the slightest attempt to free her. She was abandoned by all men. She never received from anybody even one token of sympathy. She was like Christ, utterly forsaken. At the same time, the king and others who could have helped her adored Christ in their sanctuaries. This has been true also in modern times, under the Nazis and the Communists.

*   *
*

Christians should weep with those who weep, but above all they should console Christ with their tears of sympathy.

St. Thérèse of Lisieux said: "It is for *us* to console our Lord, and not for Him to console us. His heart is so tender that if you cry, He will dry your tears. But thereafter he will go away sad, since you did not suffer Him to repose with tranquillity within you. Our Lord loves the glad of heart, the children that greet Him with a smile. When will you learn to hide your troubles from Him or to tell Him gaily that you are glad to suffer for Him?" When St. Thérèse got up in the morning, she would put the crucifix on her pillow while she dressed and say, "My Jesus, you have toiled and wept enough in your three and thirty years on this miserable earth. Rest you, today! It is my turn to suffer and fight". "Let us give our Lord pleasure. Let us by self-sacrifice give Him souls!"

St. Thérèse of Lisieux once reproached a nun for complaining so much about her troubles to her sisters. The nun answered, "You are right. Such was my own thought. Henceforth my tears will be for God alone. I shall confide my worries to One, who will understand and console me". To which St. Thérèse replied, "Tears for God! That must not be! Far less to Him than to His creatures ought you to show a mournful face".

*   *
*

At the Last Judgment, nobody will be asked how much he suffered but only how much he loved.

St. Maria Goretti, who was stabbed by a murderer, said while dying, "I wish to have him near me in paradise". This murderer, who had become a Christian in prison, attended the ceremony of beatification for the same Maria.

Christians, while suffering at the hand of enemies, love them.

They can do so because they have before their eyes the great innocent Sufferer—Jesus.

* *
*

A Christian also becomes a ruthless fighter. Look only at Martin Luther in his great struggle.

And a Christian is no quitter. He will fight to the end all the enemies of love and truth.

A Christian never submits to his enemies. I knew a Christian in a solitary cell where there was room for only three steps to and fro. He never made three steps but only two. He—not his jailors—decided what he had to do.

* *
*

We have an example of a fighting spirit in Jesus. He knew that the priests and rulers would send the multitude to arrest Him in Gethsemane. He who recommended that others flee in times of danger Himself stood by.

Not only this. Sometimes He was very aggressive, as for instance when He drove out the merchants from the temple. Then, too, His disciples were armed. They were armed becaused He willed it so.

The state motto of Virginia (U.S.A.) consists of the words of Brutus as he drove his knife into Caesar: "Sic semper tyrannis" (so alway to tyrants). This was the spirit in which Jesus had lived from childhood and which He passed on to His disciples. The only holy book which He left them was the Old Testament, a book of epic and hard fights.

But the truth is always dual in nature. On the other hand, you see in Jesus a great leniency toward the wicked. He recommends, for example, that they not be uprooted but allowed to grow together with the good until the time of the Last Judgment.

This does not mean that Jesus ever abandons the fight. But a marksman levels his gun at a point higher than the target.

The wicked man is driven by a force over which he has no control, the power of sin. Sometimes you have to fight hostile

E

men as such. You have to fight men who keep you from ful-filling your duty. The Satan about whom Paul complains in I Thessalonians 2:18 for putting obstacles in the way of his preaching might very well have had a human name. But the Christian fight is not so much a fight against men as a fight against Satan and against sin, which is not primarily a stain on the soul but a betrayal of a friend, Jesus. Our fight is against principalities, against powers, against the rulers of the darkness of this world, against spiritual wickedness in high places.

* *

*

We have to fight against pride.

After washing the feet of His disciples, Jesus dried them. Wet feet show that the feet were dirty and needed to be washed. Dry feet show simply that they are clean. Jesus does not wish us to be washed sinners, but clean men!

We too are called to wash away the sins of others in all humility. St. John of the Cross said, "Where there is no love, place love, and you will find love".

* *

*

Jesus served even more than was needed. His simple death would have been enough to atone for our sins. But He took upon Himself sufferings which were not prophesied—as, for instance, the crown of thorns—so that even if you have com-mitted the most surprising sins and crimes, crimes yet un-equalled and known by nobody, you might be very sure that the sacrifice of Jesus is enough to save you from those crimes.

Since He humbled Himself to the uttermost, you must fight your pride to the uttermost.

We should do more for Him than we are asked. The ser-vant who does only the things demanded of him is called by Jesus unprofitable. When He wished to enter into Jerusalem, He humbly asked for a donkey to sit on. Today Christians fly with jets and drive with cars to proclaim Him. Do not restrict your vision! Magnify Him, which means, make Him bigger! Do not make Him always sit on an ass, do not make of Him the God of a small confession, of one race, of one nation, or of one religious point of view!

God had ordered that His temple be a tent. David gave more than God demanded. He decided that God must have a palace for a temple.

Christ also did not only everything God commanded Him to do for our salvation—He did more.

*　　　*

*

While fighting, the Christian yet serves with gentleness. What Jesus praised most in Matthew 26:10-13 was a woman's act, a poetic gesture, that served no useful purpose. In the end, what is the use of the sufferings of martyrs? If they had been clever, they could have prevaricated and survived. But there is beauty in sacrifice, not utility. Beauty is appreciated by Jesus.

Lead your fights beautifully!

*　　　*

*

Fight without fear, knowing that the ship of Christ navigates contrary to the law of hydrodynamics. It can float even when it is full of water. (Luke 8:23). At that point the calming of the tempest by Jesus did not make any difference. Ships full of water drown even when the sea is quiet. The advance of the church is a continuous miracle.

*　　　*

*

We have to fight to win souls. Jesus said that we should be fishers of men. Now let us begin by trying to catch the greatest Fish. The symbol of Jesus in the first centuries was the fish, called in Greek Ichtys, a word composed of the initials of the words "Jesus Christ, Son of God, Saviour" in Greek.

Let us catch this great Fish, and then we will have other fishes, too.

*　　　*

*

After having suffered for us, Jesus was resurrected and ascended to heaven, where he was crowned. He had emptied Himself to become a man. Now He is again on the throne of God.

God identifies Himself with us. In Hebrew and in Greek, it is not written "the God of Abraham and of Isaac and of Jacob" but simply "the God Abraham, Isaac and Jacob". He is a God who has identified Himself with us. If He is crowned, we are crowned. "Isaac" means in Hebrew "he will laugh". He is a God who has victory in His pocket. He is the God Isaac. He will laugh.

He takes our names, even if they are sometimes ridiculous, like the name of Jacob, which means "holding by the heel".

No one has so stained himself with sin that God would not be ready to identify with him. You can be crowned together with Jesus! And then you will lead the life of a crowned being, a life of happiness.

There exists a God whose name is "God Abraham, God Isaac". One of His names is "God Richard". The church fathers said that God has all names. God through His church wishes to identify with men.

When I first read the New Testament thoroughly, it seemed to me a ridiculous book. St. Paul writes about having been crucified and buried with Jesus and about being seated in heavenly places, assertions which could not possibly be true.

Paul had not been crucified with Jesus. Jesus died between two thieves, and that was all. Paul could not have been buried. Whoever has been laid in a tomb dead does not write epistles about this experience. When he wrote that he was seated in heavenly places, he was seated in a prison cell. How can a book considered holy by millions of good minds contain such fantasies or outright lies?

The answer to my puzzle I found in St. Thomas Aquinas. He says, "Actiones et passiones sunt suppositorum". (Actions and passions belong to the person.) It is not my stomach that is hungry, but *I*. *I* walk, not my legs. *I* think, not my brain. Every member of mine is me. *I* am healthy, sick, rich, poor.

I die. The whole person is involved in every action and passion.

Now, Christians belong to one great body, Jesus Christ. Just as I am hurt if you kick my shins, so Christ is hurt or caressed in the things which are done to us, His members. Do not believe that I speak about Christians constituting the body of Christ in some mystical sense. St. Paul writes, "We are members of his body". This could be interpreted in a spiritual sense. He adds "[members] of his flesh". This perhaps could also be spiritualized. (What can an exegete not spiritualize?) So, to be very sure, he emphasizes his meaning, "We are members of his body, of his flesh, *and of his bones*" (Eph. 5:30).

I am a member of His body. I am involved in everything which has happened and now happens to Him. I have been crucified and buried with Him. I am seated with Him in heavenly places. I will return with Him in glory. He is with me in my daily life. Luther says rightly, "The Christian is Christ". I identify myself with Him, He with me. Our religion is one without pronouns.

*　　　*

*

Knowing that they are crowned together with Jesus, Christians need fear no one, because fear, the soul's greatest enemy apart from sin itself, will have disappeared.

We can be calm in all things. As you grow old, you do not have to ask yourself what you will do in your old age, but what God will do with your old age. If you come to a great age, He will make your age *be* great.

*　　　*

*

Crowned with Jesus, you can fulfil the words of St. Bernard of Clairvaux: "Let your ears fast from rumours, praise, slander, gossip, controversy, and your tongue fast from detraction, murmuring, faultfinding".

The serenity of the crowned believer resists in the most difficult circumstances.

In a Siberian prison, Catholic nuns refused to lay down their garbs and take up the prison uniform, which they considered to be the sign of the Antichrist. So they were taken to the bathroom, and while they were in the bath, their garments were changed. When they emerged and still refused to put on the prison uniform, they were forced to sit out in the cold, where the temperature was forty below zero. Undaunted, they began to say their prayers. The woman doctor of the prison, a Jewish Trotskyite, told them, "You are committing suicide". They did not answer but continued their prayers. Even when the male warders entered, the sixty nuns did not move. The director of the prison feared to bring in Communist youth to dress them by force because he was afraid they would be contaminated by the courage of these nuns.

By this time the shivering women were blue with the cold. Naked, they were driven over the snow to their cells. A major, director of the prison, said: "It was easier to fight with the Nazis than these nuns".

Each nun passing the major bowed to him, saying, "May God forgive you". Some of them could no longer walk and were supported by others.

So they ran over the snow, singing the "Our Father" in the old Gregorian melody. Not one of them fell sick. In their cells, they dressed themselves with some rags from other prisoners. They had been six hours in the cold.

A second woman doctor asked the Jewess, Doctor Bravermann, "How do you explain the fact from a medical point of view that not one of them fell sick?" The atheist Jewish doctor answered, "They have explained it themselves by singing the words, 'Our Father who art in heaven'."

*   *

*

Crowned with Jesus, you are free from the worry of calculating results. You quietly follow your impulses, knowing that the law of God is written in your new heart.

70

You know that God is as much your Father as He was the Father of Jesus Christ, and that He cares for every detail of your life.

In Deuteronomy 16:6-7, God commands that at Passover the Jews, His chosen people, eat a lamb. A lamb can be prepared in many ways: it can be grilled, fried, broiled, cooked. But surely roasted lamb is the best kind, and you see that in verse seven God cares even about such a detail and recommends how the lamb should be prepared in order to appeal to the taste. He acts as if He were chief waiter in a big restaurant who wishes to recommend what to eat. So He says, "Thou shalt roast the lamb".

*　　*

*

When you know that you are sustained by such a God, everything around you becomes beautiful.

Only the Bible comes from God—not the titles in the Bibles. You sense this immediately. Jesus tells a parable about a man who sowed good wheat in his field, only to have an enemy come and sow tares. In the end, the tares were burned and the good wheat was taken into the barn. Angels made the determination. The title in the Bible is "The parable of the tares". Why it is not "of the wheat and the tares"?

Jesus tells a parable about ninety-nine sheep that remained faithful and one that was lost. This is called by men "The parable of the lost sheep".

Jesus tells another parable about a good father and his two sons, one of whom remained with the father, while the other left with his inheritance, squandered it, and then returned home. This is called "The parable of the prodigal son". Why not "The parable of the good father" or "The parable of the repenting son"?

The titles have not been well chosen.

The children of God should look for what is beautiful and true, because their souls and minds have been purified through

71

the hygiene of worship. They should avoid such misleading titles.

* *
*

Being crowned with Jesus, you can lead a life full of love. You risk nothing in loving without being loved. That is how Christ loved us. Though despised and forsaken, He yet became Lord of all.

If you have reached this point in life, stay with it!

A certain son was a very great lover of nature. With much difficulty, he succeeded in convincing his comfort-loving father to climb on a hill during a walk. From the top of the hill the son, much moved, exclaimed, "Look, father, how beautiful it is down below!" To which the father angrily replied, "You drove me to this height in order to make me see how beautiful it is down below?"

Do not look back! Do not look into the valley from which you have come.

Crowned with Jesus, you have arrived at the very peak. Stay there and look up.

* *
*

If you believe in the crowned Jesus, you can accept what every day brings you, since your days are preordained by a loving God.

In John 18:31–32, we read that the Jews did not wish to execute Jesus according to their own laws, which prescribed punishment by stoning. They decided rather that He should be crucified and not stoned. They believed that they did this of their own free will, not realizing their decision had actually been foreordained. They shouted "Crucify him!" so that the words of Jesus might be fulfilled, which He spoke, signifying what death He should die.

So all things are foreordained in our lives. We are like people viewing a movie. Once I surprised myself in a theatre by praying for someone on the screen, an innocent man in deadly danger, but the outcome had long since been decided. It was "foreordained" on the reel in the operator's booth.

*   *
*

We live favoured lives. Christians not only do not have free will. By virtue of their being Christians they agree beforehand with everything that is in God's plan for them. Like angels, they simply fulfil God's decisions.

As fire changes into fire everything thrown into it, so God changes into Godhead everyone who approaches Him. The will of God and the will of the individual become one in purpose, while remaining two wills.

*   *
*

Christians welcome brother Death.

My body has had many shapes: that of a foetus, that of a babe, of a child, of an adult, of an old man. It has sometimes been healthy, sometimes sick. Why should I worry about the fact that the body will take the shape of a corpse? I am not my body; I will remain. I am indestructible.

In Amos 8:2, the Lord says to the prophet: "The end is come upon my people of Israel". But here, even the almightyness of God has a limit. Not even He could destroy the people of Israel. This people is safe.

*   *
*

To die does not mean to disappear. It means to leave through one door and enter another.

Believing in the crowned Jesus, our hearts become quiet. God can shut the many doors surrounding us but never the one above us.

*   *
*

Believing in the crowned Jesus, you have a right to holy communion. One such communion is worth all the troubles of a lifetime.

Christians are members of the body of Christ, flesh of His flesh and bone of His bones. He is the high priest. The whole high priest, head and body, stands before God. Christ, who sacrified His earthly body on Calvary two thousand years ago, now sacrifices His mystical body in the cross-burdened lives of the believers. Christ is represented on the communion table. The Christian is Christ. We are also in the bread and in the chalice. So are all our brethren from all ages and all places, even the frailest ones.

From the sacrifice of her Chief, commemorated in holy communion, the church learns to sacrifice herself and all her possessions.

At holy communion, the one who officiates and the communicants must also say of themselves, "This is my body, . . . this is my blood, shed for the remission of sins".

St. Cyprian wrote, "The sacrifice of our Saviour is not celebrated with the required sanctity if our offering of ourselves does not correspond to his passion".

St. Augustine taught, "God knows nothing better, all-powerful though He be, God can do nothing more precious than the most holy eucharist" (the ancient name for holy communion).

Catholics and Orthodox on one side and Protestants on the other have debated for centuries the question of trans-substantiation, that is whether the bread and wine actually become the body and blood of Jesus Christ. It would be much more important to believe that we are trans-substantiated, that our bodies are really His and that His blood circulates through our veins. Then our lives would be godly, strengthened by the reminder of holy communion.

*   *

*

You have the saving, the suffering, the serving, the fighting, the crowned Jesus.

Therefore you can cry defiantly to your passions that though they conquer you a million times, they will never vanquish you, that you will crush them in the end however long the

74

struggle may be. The essence of the Christian religion is not winning, but daring. Jesus is the way, not only the prize.

* *
*

What should you do to lead a victorious life?

Generally speaking, the question "What should I do?" has no place in the Christian religion. There is no answer to it, because the question is wrong. No matter how much you do, you can never repay the gifts of God. With how much would you pay for having eyes? The Christian simply says, "I have received countless gifts, and I have confidence that the One who has been so generous toward me till now will continue to give. He will give victory, too".

The Christian also avoids wishing for what God does not give. Temporary riches are gained by requiring, spiritual gifts by renouncing.

Simple trust in God and renunciation of what He does not give will assure one of victory.

The Christian has no goals of his own to attain. He is passively at the disposal of God. Therefore, he is sanctified without being strained. Strain exists only when one is goaded on by ambition. But your sanctification is not your ambition. It is God's ambition for you. You will attain it by being relaxed.

* *
*

When you become a Christian you begin a new chapter in your life. Musicians tune their instruments before playing. Do the same! You will have to play a different kind of music.

* *
*

Young David, a shepherd boy, was brought to the court o: king Saul and soon became everybody's favourite. Once, wher. the court was assembled, he asked the king's permission to play a harp which the king had near his throne. The king replied, "No use! I have been deceived by the one who made it for me. Nobody could ever play on it. It produces only discord".

75

David insisted. When he touched the cords of the harp with his fingers, lo, the instrument began to rejoice and weep and rejoice again at his command. The music he played was so glorious that when he finished, everyone was in tears.

The king asked him, "How is it that all the others could not play on this harp and you could?" David answered, "All the others tried to play their own songs on the harp, and the harp refused to obey. I have played to the harp its own song. I reminded her of the beautiful times when she was a young tree in the forest, when birds chirped in her branches and her leaves were bathed in sun—and you heard the joy of the harp. Then I told her of my sympathy for the suffering through which she passed on the terrible day when men cut down the tree. But its death had not been in vain. For out of its wood a harp was made, on which God's praises could be played. And the harp rejoiced when she understood her calling".

When the Messiah comes, many will try to play their own songs on His harp. The result will be a Christianity of terrible ugliness. But there will always be the chosen ones who will play His songs, the song of His eternal glory, the song of His humiliation in becoming a babe in a manger, the song of His life of sorrow, the song of Calvary, the song of His resurrection and ascension.

Tune your instrument for playing His songs!

*   *

*

In "The parable of the tares" Jesus teaches that the devil can imitate God well. He can sow tares so similar to the good wheat that even the elect cannot be trusted to distinguish rightly between them.

Never trust your own judgment in matters of faith. Christ has instituted the church as a fellowship which should establish the rules of Christian behaviour according to the Word of God. It is not right to do what you consider right. You can be honestly deceived.

By believing in Jesus, you enter into the communion of saints. You are in communion with the saints of old, such as

St. Paul and Silvanus, who continue to give thanks in heaven for your faith (I Thess. 2). You are in communion with the saints of all ages as well as those who are your contemporaries.

I have told you to leave the disciples in order to come to Jesus. Once you are His, seek the disciples.

*   *

*

The church has a code of rules, but it is not fixed in all matters. It has changed many times throughout history. Except for the main tenets of behaviour, the church leaves the decision for your Christian life to your own conscience enlightened by the Word of God. Spiritual guides who claim to know all the answers to every individual case prove by this that they are false teachers. The true teacher says about many things, "I do not know".

*   *

*

You will have to make your own decisions even in very big matters. There is such a thing as a moral relativism.

Even the commandment "Do not kill" is not absolute. Not every killing is wrong. How mankind would have been benefited if a plot against Hitler at an early stage had succeeded.

But the church knows about such extraordinary circumstances, too. As a member of the church, you drive on well established rails. The great lines of behaviour, including the possibility of exceptions, are fixed. The church has wise pastors. Take your own decisions, but consult them. One of the best decisions you could make is to obey your pastor.

*   *

*

The church has had and still has many true saints.

I will tell a few episodes from the lives of these saints. Some of them will seem extravagant. But exceptional men cannot be judged by ordinary standards. They are different from anyone else.

*   *

*

The governor asked St. Justin the Martyr, "Listen, you so-called man of the Word, believed to possess true wisdom: if you were scourged and executed now, do you believe you would enter into heaven?" Justin answered, "I trust firmly that I will live there if I endure all this. I am full of this certitude". The governor threatened him again, only to be told again, "Our ardent desire is to suffer for our Lord Jesus Christ and then to be saved".

* *

*

The man now known as St. Anthony the Great once heard in church the familiar verse, "If thou wilt be perfect, go and sell that thou hast, and give to the poor, and come and follow me". (Matt. 19:21). Anthony, as if alone in the church, knew the words were addressed to him. Jesus had uttered them and the evangelist had recorded them for him. Anthony straightway went out and got rid of his 120 acres of land and 300 sheep. Everything went to the poor. He induced his sister to follow suit. She became a nun, he a monk.

Bread, salt and water were his diet once a day; sometimes once a week. He lived in a ruined castle on the top of a mountain. Every six months, bread was brought. There he stayed some twenty years.

Every night was passed in prayer. Once he admonished the rising sun, "Why do you turn me from contemplating the splendour of the true Light?"

After twenty years of meditation, he re-entered active life. During the persecution of Maximin, he journeyed to Alexandria to comfort the imprisoned faithful. (In our day not one single church leader has thought to do such a thing.) He visited the convicts condemned to work the mines in the Sudan.

He hid St. Athanasius from his persecutors.

Once in a vision the saint had seen the earth covered with so many devilish snares that it seemed impossible for anyone to escape falling into them. He asked God how they could be avoided. He was answered by one word—*humility*.

*   *

*

A man who was a widower decided to enter the monastery. He had an only daughter who insisted that she go with him, disguised as a man, so that she might care for him. She was received among the monks. She enchanted all the brethren through her voice and her skill in cooking and washing. Believed to be a man, she won the confidence of the abbot. He sent her together with two other monks into town for the purpose of shopping. Now the innkeeper at whose establishment they were accustomed to stay had a daughter. She became pregnant after an affair with a soldier, who did not wish to marry her. In despair, she asked, "What will I do? Father will kill me!" He replied, "Tell him that this young nice monk raped you". This is what she did.

When Theodora (this was the name of the monk) returned from town, the abbot, who by now had received a complaint from the father, was ready to beat him. "How could you bring such shame upon our monastery?" he thundered. Theodora was afraid that one of the other monks might have committed the sin. She knew that, if found guilty, he would be expelled from the monastery and might fall into even worse sins. So she fell on her knees before the abbot and said, "Forgive me, all my gross sins". The abbot drove her out. She lived as a beggar at the gate of the monastery, bowing to every monk who passed by with the words, "Forgive me, a miserable sinner".

After many years, the abbot pardoned her. She could re-enter the monastery but was put to the most menial tasks and was despised by all. When she died, her body had to be washed. Then it was discovered that she had been a girl and that she had covered somebody else's sins.

Since that time, she has been honoured as St. Theodora.

*   *

*

St. Paphnutius sold himself as a slave to a comedian with the sole aim of converting him. The conversion took twenty years, whereupon the comedian set him free. So he sold himself in order to relieve the hardships of a poor widow.

When released the second time, he was given a cloak, a tunic, and a gospel as presents. The cloak went to the first beggar, the tunic to the second. It was easy to do this. But how could he keep a gospel when there were so many poor people? He sold it and gave away this money, too.

Nothing but dry bread and water ever entered his mouth, and little besides Scripture ever came out of it.

*   *
*

St. Cyprian wrote to the imprisoned Christians of his time, "You have no garments on your body and only a little bread as food, but you are clothed with Christ in glory. Man does not live on bread alone".

*   *
*

The motto of St. John Chrysostom was, "Glory to God for all things". He finished his letters from exile with these words. After being dragged by soldiers through the winter snow, he died in a little wayside church. His last words while lying on the cold stone floor were, "Glory to God for all things".

*   *
*

Thais had been a courtesan in Egypt. St. Serapion, a monk, converted her. He had put on normal clothes and had waited in line as if to receive her favours. She was so impressed with his words that she forthwith burned her furniture, dresses, and all the accoutrements of other luxury. Serapion took her to a convent, where he kept her three years in a cell with a sealed door. Her diet was bread and water. The whole time she said just one prayer: "You who have made me, save me".

At the end of the three years, the monk had a vision, in which he saw a splendid mansion prepared in heaven. He was sure that it was for St. Anthony, but a voice told him, "This place is for Thais". Serapion unsealed her door. After fifteen days, she passed away.

In 1899, excavations uncovered her cell and that of Serapion, with inscriptions which made their identification possible.

*   *

*

Old Zosimus saw in the wilderness a naked being. She cried from afar, "I am a woman. Throw me your mantle to cover myself". She confessed to him that she had led a shameful life all during her youth. At one time she went to a big Christian festival in Jerusalem to engage in her profession. While there, she came to her senses and asked Christ to obtain for her the grace of repentance. Since then, she said, she had spent 47 years in the desert, eating berries and herbs. Her clothes had fallen to pieces.

She asked Zosimus to return the next year with holy communion. She took communion, sang, "Lord, now lettest thou thy servant depart in peace . . .," and begged the priest to return in Lent. But this time he found her dead.

You will have recognized the story of St. Mary the Egyptian.

*   *

*

Robbers broke into the cell of St. Macarius and then spoiled the monastery, too. He assisted them, carrying out divers things which they had overlooked.

On another occasion, he caught thieves stealing into the cell of a fellow monk. He warned them to move on before they got caught.

*   *

*

St. Polycarp, when faced with the alternative of being devoured by wild beasts or of denying Christ, said, "Fourscore and six years have I been His servant and He has done me no wrong. How then can I blaspheme the Lord who saved me?" He died a martyr's death.

*   *

*

F

When St. Perpetua was thrown into the circus under the Roman emperors to be devoured by wild beasts, she fell and her thighs were seen. She covered them, mindful of modesty rather than of pain.

* *

*

St. Francis of Assisi during a sleepless night was persuaded that the song of a nightingale was an act of worship. So the whole night long he chanted the praises of God alternately with the bird.

* *

*

St. Thomas Moore was in prison because he refused to acknowledge that King Henry VIII, who was at that time seeking sanction for divorce and remarriage, was head of the church. The wife of Thomas reproached him, "Why should you stay in gaol full of lice and attacked by rats when all the bishops have acknowledged the king's claim to lead the church? Your house is waiting for you". He replied, "Is my house nearer to heaven than this cell? Will not the same death take me from my house, too?" He remained steadfast in his refusal and was beheaded.

* *

*

In the beginning of the past century, the bloody queen Ranavalona reigned over Madagascar. She hated Christians because they opposed the slave trade. She ordered all missionaries out of the country and commanded that all Bibles be burned. Any avowed Christian had all his property confiscated and was sold as a slave or killed.

Christians gathered in the woods. They formed underground churches. But the queen could not take away from them the Spirit of God. And they were encouraged by examples of heroism of martyrs like Rasalama, a woman who went to death singing, and others who were burnt alive rather than deny their faith. Some who were thrown from cliffs remained faithful to the end.

This persecution lasted for fifteen years.

*　　　*

*

William Wilberforce dedicated his whole public career to the cause of the slaves. And he succeeded. First he stopped ocean traffic in slaves by British ships. Then he obtained the emancipation of the slaves in the British Empire. At midnight on July 31, 1834, 800,000 slaves became free. It was Wilberforce's deed.

His whole fight was animated by the love of Christ. He said, "God Almighty has set before me the objective of suppressing slavery".

He left us this teaching: "No inner feelings ought to be taken as a demonstration of the Spirit being in any man, but only the change of disposition and conduct".

*　　　*

*

From pastor Kaj Munk, killed for his faith by the Nazis in Denmark, we have the words, "There are men who believe that you can somehow salt the truth. They suppose that you can hold it hidden in a barrel well salted and use a part of it when the need arises. But we, too, have men with a living faith that truth exists in order to be said and that it exists only when it is said. These good men are of the same stuff as John the Baptist. Like him, they sense fear for their own fate and fear even more the damages and sufferings which the naked truth can bring upon their people. But one day they realize that cowardice must not bind their tongue any more, that the sufferings which come to people because of hypocrisy, silence and lies are a thousand times more dangerous. We have also in our country a Herod, who commits incest with strange gods. I have named the spirit of compromise which does not shrink back from undignified actions for the sake of comfort".

*　　　*

*

Pastor Bonnhoeffer, a German martyred under Hitler, wrote from prison: "I have become perfectly sure of my faith. It has resisted unshattered under heavy burdens. There has never been a moment of hesitation or despair . . . However strange it may sound : I have learnt in prison to rejoice".

When called out of his cell to be executed, he uttered these words: "This is the end : the beginning of life".

* *

*

An American pastor preaching in 1954 in India was asked to participate in a service of prayer for the sick. One young woman with a wild look in her eyes refused to come into the service but kept apart, surrounded by people who said that she was demon-possessed. When the pastor endeavoured to kneel beside her, she became frantic and rolled over on her mat unconscious. He prayed in the name of Christ for her health. At the end of the prayer, she opened her eyes and they were normal and full of light. A beautiful smile came over her face as she stretched out her hands for him to lift her to her feet. She was marvellously delivered through the name of Jesus.

There are pastors who are real saints to whom God has given such power.

* *

*

David Brainerd died in the early part of the eighteenth century at the age of 29, after having borne great hardships while preaching the gospel to the American Indians.

In his diary he recorded his struggles: "I lodge on a bundle of straw, my labour is hard and extremely difficult, and I have little appearance of success to comfort me . . . The Dutch hate me because I preach to the Indians". Insinuations were brought against him as though he were training them to cut people's throats.

One August 20 he wrote: "Having lain in a cold sweat all night, I coughed much bloody matter this morning". On August 22: "Continued my course up the river . . . at night lodged in the open wood". August 24 : "Visited some of the Delaware Indians and discoursed with them about Christianity".

He has left behind a few precious thoughts:

"It is worth the while to follow after God through a thousand snares, deserts and death itself".

"God has made me willing to do anything that I can do, consistent with truth, for the sake of peace, and that I might not be a stumbling block to others. For this reason I can cheerfully forego and give up what I verily believe, after the most mature and impartial search, is my right, in some instances. God has given me that disposition that, if this were the case that a man has done me a hundred injuries and I (though ever so much provoked by it) have done him one, I feel disposed and heartily willing humbly to confess my fault to him, and on my knees to ask forgiveness of him; though at the same time he should justify himself in all the injuries he has done me and should make use of my humble confession to blacken my character the more and represent me as the only person guilty".

"Oh, it is an emblem of heaven itself to love all the world with a love of kindness, forgiveness and benevolence; to feel our souls sedate, mild and meek; to be void of all evil surmisings and suspicions and scarce able to think evil of any man upon any occasion; to find our hearts simple, open and free to those that look upon us with a different eye".

* *
*

In the Soviet Union, a pastor was led to prison, together with a teenager whom he had brought to conversion. The mother of the lad threw stones at the pastor, who turned to her and said, "I admire your motherly love".

* *
*

God is beautiful in His saints.

* *
*

You do not have to try to lead a heroic Christian life. It is as futile to try to be a hero as it is futile to try to be an elephant. Very few have the stuff of which great saints and martyrs are made.

It is good for Christians to know that in the Roman, medieval, Nazi, and Communist persecution, the majority of Christians were not ready to suffer and die for their faith. Only a minority faced torture and death with courage. But the others were also Christians. God saw how sorry they were for their weakness and how eagerly they returned to faith when the immediate danger had passed.

It is a miracle that Jesus can make at least some sheep lie down in green pastures (Ps. 23 :2). Normally, a sheep does not lie down. It will graze for hours, even if it is not hungry. How can you lie down with so much green grass around? How can you renounce the world when it offers you so many pleasures?

But among the saints are reckoned not only a St. Anthonie or a St. Paphnutius, or others who have been canonized, or those who have died in prison for their faith. An average Christian life is also a Christian life. An everyday Christian is also a saint.

*   *

*

A small dog once stood near a big Doberman. The Doberman scorned him and asked: "Do you also claim to be a dog?" The little creature did not dare to contradict the Doberman. He answered politely: "Sir, I am surely not as big a dog as you. But neither can you assert that I am a cat". Small dogs are also dogs! And small Christians are also Christians.

When my son Mihai was five years old, he worried when I read to him from the Bible that the saints will walk with Jesus clothed in white. He asked if Jesus had clothes small enough for children. I had to assure him that Jesus has white garments for all Christians, large or small in size, and large or small in faith.

86

Not all of us can perform the deeds of heroes of the faith. But we can admire, love and rejoice in them. We can battle unceasingly against the guile of oblivion which threatens the life of the hero. Mirrored in the love of the admirer, the deeds of the hero will appear even more beautiful than they were in reality. The admirer makes of the hero, who was also only human, a legend.

You must not worry that you cannot be like him. A snail and a hare can walk the same path and arrive at the same goal. It may take you more time, but you will have over the hero the advantage of longer perseverance. Every Christian is called a saint. If you cannot do better, be a saint snail!

If you cannot be the best, be second best.

In a sense an embryo is already a man. You are a great artist only if you have the gift before you have drawn a line. A Christian has Christ within, as well when he makes his first unsure steps as when he is mature in the faith.

*　　　*

*

Do not fear the great demands of the Bible. They might overwhelm you, as for instance the words of Jesus: "Be ye therefore perfect, even as your Father which is in heaven is perfect". These express a desire. What professor of music does not desire that all his pupils be future Wagners and Beethovens? But life does not work out this way. Nobody becomes a genius by willing, nor an exceptional saint.

Spurgeon used to tell a story: A man was renowned for his orchard in which grew the best apples of the world. His friend, however, was unconvinced because several times he had passed by the orchard, had picked up out of curiosity a few apples that had fallen from the trees, and had found them to be sour and tasteless. Therefore he repeatedly refused the invitations of the owner to have a look at his orchard. Finally, the owner insisted on knowing the reason, and his friend told him his experience. The owner laughed: "Knowing that I have the best apples in my orchard, I was faced with the problem of how to protect them from thieves and children.

So I planted around the fence two or three rows of worthless apple trees. These discourage theft. As for my guests, they are taken to the inner orchard where they can taste apples of unparalleled quality and aroma".

Jesus has done likewise. He has for His guests the best of gifts, a quiet reliance on His sacrifice, which is effective without human deeds and virtues. But to prevent hypocrites from taking advantage of this, He has surrounded His property with a few trees which yield very sour apples.

It is a sour apple for those who are not among God's elect to hear that they have to be perfect as the Father in heaven is perfect, that they have to take up their cross daily, that they have to mortify their flesh.

The children of God do not enter into Jesus' garden this way. They enter by the royal gate and are happy to be saved without any effort on their part, but just by what Christ has done for them.

* *
*

We have the precious gift of being beloved without any merit of our own, just as little children are beloved by their parents.

It does not matter how much in the Christian life we are able to accomplish. God looks only at the will. Kierkegaard said that purity of heart is to will one thing, and Christians surely will this one thing. Every Christian is a model of the good and the true : he is so in his intentions.

His ideals are high. He wills always to be at the peak. It is said about the sculptor Phideas that he worked with very great care on the back of a statue of the goddess Dianna, which was to stand in a niche. He was asked : "But who will see in there?" He answered : "The gods". We try to do all things well, that God might have pleasure. We also know that we have a God who understands our weakness. The beginning of godliness in us makes us pleasant to God.

We have time to achieve our ideals. Christians are never in a hurry. In Matthew 27:52 it is written that when Jesus died the graves were opened and many bodies of the saints which slept arose. But even in these circumstances, they were in no hurry at all. They came out of their graves only after His resurrection, which means the third day. You recognize those who are eternal by the fact that they take their time.

*   *

*

A rabbi asked a Jew: "What would you do if you found a wallet on the street containing much money, along with the owner's card?" The Jew answered: "To tell you the truth, rabbi, I have many children and am poor. I would consider it a gift from God". The rabbi told him: "You are a thief". The rabbi put the same question to a second Jew. His reply was: "I would restore the money immediately". The rabbi told him: "You are an idiot". He asked a third Jew, who said: "I know what my duty would be. I know my weakness. I could not say what I would do in such circumstances. Everything depends upon the grace of God". The rabbi praised him: "This is the right answer".

We know it is our Christian duty to be perfect. We know our inability to be so. We are in every moment of our lives what grace makes us.

*   *

*

Svetlana Alliluyeva, the daughter of Stalin, writes that in the Soviet Union everybody has to learn to lie from early childhood in order to survive. Otherwise one is crushed by the tyranny.

Happily, it is not so in the free world. But life would not be possible anywhere if you were always to tell everyone the naked truth. Neither can you go around decrying the falsity of all attitudes, you consider erroneous. Rather, you must be with Paul be a Jew to the Jews and a Greek to the Greeks in order to achieve something for the Lord Jesus and to bring men to Him.

Leave the absolutes to those specially equipped by God to deal with them!

*   *

*

Absolutes cannot be applied always and by all in time of war. The church is at war. In a war, you must not be idealistic with regard to the means you use, but effective.

It is said that Sir Stafford Cripps, on hearing one of the radio broadcasts of the British psychological warfare branch, remarked: "If we have to resort to this sort of thing to win the war, I had rather we lost it". Let people who think like this not enter the war! Whoever wishes to clean a dirty place must be ready to get himself dirty.

Fortunately, Great Britain had not only a Sir Stafford Cripps, but also a Churchill and many others who thought like him.

While General Montgomery was putting the final touches to the D-day plans in London, a double of Montgomery was sent from Gibraltar to Algiers to deceive the German spies. Hitler was disarmed: Montgomery is not even in England, so probably an invasion of France is not imminent.

The German battleship Graf Spee was in for repairs only 48 hours in Montevideo. It was not allowed to stay longer in a neutral harbour. But lying in wait were only two small British ships, which it could easily defeat. The nearest British warships were too far away to arrive in time. Then the admiralty resorted to deception. They sent to their small British ship a signal that a big battleship and aircraft were joining them. They knew that the German admiralty and German captain would break the code. In fact, they purposely used a code that could be broken. As a result, the German captain Langdorff sank his ship and committed suicide.

We see the same thing in Judges 20:29: "Israel set liers in wait round about Gibeah" in order to ambush the children of Benjamin. Then when the Benjamites went out against the people of Israel, they were drawn away from the city and made to believe that their enemies were smitten down before

90

them. The children of Israel pretended to flee, so as to draw them further away from the city into the highways, and then at a certain moment the liers in wait of Israel came forth out of their hiding places. So Benjamin was smitten.

It takes cunning to win a war. It takes cunning to win the Christian war, too.

*   *

*

Nobody is asked to lead a Christian life without compromise.

But a Christian is very conscious of the fact that these compromises, though necessary sometimes in life and in a fight, are also very dangerous. There is no lie without injury to someone's faith in what another says. Necessarily, society is injured by every instance of lying.

A man asked a traveller through the desert to allow him to ride on the back of his camel. The request was granted. Once mounted, the man threw the owner of the camel into the sand and fled. The owner cried after him: "I am not troubled that you took my camel. I have others. But you have destroyed faith between men. In future, camel owners will not help lonely travellers. Nobody will be allowed any more on the back of the camel".

A Christian takes such facts into account. He never says an untruth because he wills it, but because the necessities of a holy fight impose this burden upon him. Nuns hid Jewesses, sought by the Nazis in order to be burned, and lied when asked saying they did not know where they were.

*   *

*

The question of compromise in Christian life does not refer only to saying the truth but to a whole range of problems. Let us not forget that the disciples of Jesus were armed. Peter had a sword on him. Jesus did not rebuke him for this but only for using it at the wrong time, though he surely knew the danger of being armed. Homer says: "The sword itself often provokes a man to fight".

So we will have compromises in different spheres of life.

91

But if we do not recognize other absolutes, neither do we recognize an absolute necessity of compromising. Withal, there must be a steadfast clinging to principles.

If every bad man can master his good desires, why should we not be able to master our bad passions?

*   *

*

Not too much will be demanded of you. It would have been nice if the shepherds who went to see the baby Jesus had brought a little bit of butter, cheese and milk for the hungry family. You will be taught to do such little practical things. —

Every letter you write can become an ambassador of love.

*   *

*

One of the rules of the Bible in moral matters is continued in Ecclesiastes 7:16: "Be not righteous over much".

Exaggerated honesty can be exaggerated stupidity. I know about a Christian who had in his office desk two pencils, one his own and one belonging to the company. All personal notes he made with his personal pencil, and those of the company with the company's. He stole the company's time to choose between these two pencils.

The man who will not act or speak except in total righteousness achieves nothing. He does not enter the path of progress, and he is not true because he is not real.

Christianity will make you wise in everyday living. You will know how to give the devil an opportunity to flee. If you cut away from him the possibility of withdrawal, you force him to resistance.

*   *

*

A teacher once asked his class: "What is religion?" A child gave this answer: "It is the set of things which are forbidden". Flee such a religion as you would flee from a rattlesnake!

Life is not possible without a certain amount of accommodation. We sometimes have to do things which normally would be forbidden. Blaise Pascal wrote: "Whosoever wishes to play the angel becomes a devil". Even as a Christian, remain a man! Be a saint, but—for the sake of those around you—be a human saint.

Christians have been made kings. Every king who ruled according to inflexible principles would ruin his country.

*   *
*

Christians have great promises from God, some of which go so far as to say that fire will not burn nor water drown us. These promises are fulfilled daily by the fact that God gives us the wisdom to keep away from fire and deep waters.

*   *
*

You have to coat bitter medicine with sugar to make it acceptable to children. You are surrounded by children, in mind if not in body. When Count von Zinzendorf came to the United States, he found that people had a tremendous respect for the clergy. They would not learn religion from a man who was not ordained. So he introduced himself with the title "pastor", which no man had given him. (Neither had any man given to Paul the title of apostle. He had it from God.) Beethoven would never have been accepted into higher social circles because he did not belong to the nobility, so he put before his name the word "van". "Van Beethoven" sounded like the title of a Dutch nobleman. Thus he succeeded. Perhaps his symphonies would not have come to us without this trick.

When King Pedro of Brazil wished to erect the first public hospital in his country, he appealed in vain for funds. Then he made it known that whoever gave one million pesos would get the title of a duke, whoever gave half a million would be a count, whoever 100,000 would be a baron. In no time, he had all the money needed. The hospital was built. All the notables were gathered when the commemorative plate was to be unveiled. It bore the inscription: "This hospital has been given to human suffering by human stupidity and pride".

If you wish to achieve things for Christ, pay your tribute,

with a smile of understanding, to human childishness. You are a child of God through Jesus. Others are not. You do not communicate with others on the same level of maturity.

If you are a child of God, be aware, without being proud about it, that you have only men to speak down to.

*   *

*

At the same time, recognize that you too are a sinful man. With authority Peter reproaches the Jews: "Ye denied the holy one". He also had denied Him. This is the paradox of Christian life. We reprove others for sins we commit ourselves.

Do not be surprised at anybody else's sin, not even at great sins in those whom you admire as stars in the spiritual sky.

Luther and Calvin were very far from being models of Christian love. There were stains on their characters as big as those of the popes and bishops against whom they fought. There were dark sides in the lives of Wesley and Livingstone. These have been bitterly denounced by their adversaries. The Baptist Union of Britain did not find it easy to cope with their greatest preacher, Charles Spurgeon.

If you do not accept these facts of life, you will wear yourself out in useless conflict with the unchangeable laws of existence.

Do not struggle to amend the unalterable tendencies of your own nature. Just yield to Jesus. Do not compose your life. Let Jesus compose it. Believe only that He has taken over control and give play to your feelings. He will take care to allow you as much sin as you need to be kept humble; He will give you as much righteousness as you need to shine before men.

The ordinary man has to choose which things to do and which not to do. About Abraham it is written that "God was with him in *all* that he did" (Gen. 21:22). This is your privilege if you are a child of Abraham by faith.

Some men have to choose where to go and where not to go. Joshua hears the words: "The Lord thy God is with thee *whithersoever* thou goest".

*   *

*

I have mentioned above the inconsistencies of great preachers. Soon I will pass away. It is probable that I will be completely forgotten. If not, some future author will give my sins as an example in his book to encourage those who have fallen, to show them that even a man who suffered much and preached in many countries, as a certain Richard Wurmbrand did, had great blots upon his character.

I have been accused by adversaries of the Gospel, but also by some Christian leaders, of very great sins and also of grave errors in doctrine. Miriam and Aaron, sister and brother of Moses, spoke against him. Aaron was the high priest ordained by God. Their accusations could not be discarded lightly. They knew Moses well. I, too, had men very near to me pointing their finger at me.

Some future biographer may sort these things out and find that the one or the other accusation has been factual, or he may find that my sins are in quite another sphere. To a few really bad features in my life, some will be added by adversaries. With a little ingenuity, you can make any criminal look like a saint, and vice versa. Even in the best of lives, there is much that can be read amiss deliberately. But there is residual evil which is always present in the life of every man.

When you read about evil in me and are certain of it, do not wonder. Accept sin as a fact in Wurmbrand's life, too, and praise God who had pity on such a sinner. Remember that the most beautiful book of the Bible is a song written by one of the sorriest characters of the Bible, King Solomon. Some even doubt his salvation.

*   *

*

Great preachers failed. A man of much lesser importance, Wurmbrand, has failed too. Jesus, before departing from among us, left his cause without fear or misgiving to Peter who had failed.

Archbishop Cranmer failed in his years of compromising with a tyrant. When arrested, he first recanted. He went to the stake for Christ only after wavering.

St. Joan of Arc also recanted at first.

Bismarck, at the end of his life, confessed that he had failed, that all he had done had brought happiness to not one human being.

We all live and will be saved only by grace.

* *

*

You will never have peace until you accept the first postulate of dialectics, that there is nothing that does not contain contradictions. There exists no mathematics without plus and minus, no events without actions and reactions, no electricity without a positive and a negative pole, no war without offence and defence, no saint without sins and no sinner without virtues.

Accept yourself with your contradictions. Luther said that every Christian is "simul justus et peccator, comprehensor et viator" — "simultaneously righteous and sinful, a man who has reached the goal and one who reaches out towards it".

Contradiction is universal and absolute.

* *

*

Never abandon a fearless fight! Think only about Pharaoh: how many plagues he resisted! And you, child of God, fear that you will not resist temptations?

You will surely overcome evil, but sometimes you have to take it slowly.

St. Francis of Assisi knew that some robbers surrounded his monastery and robbed from people who came to worship. The other monks wished to call the police to arrest them. St. Francis told them not to do so. He proposed that they go to the robbers with some food and wine and obtain from them a promise not to kill, but only to steal. After a time he got them to promise never to steal on Sundays or feast days. And so, slowly, slowly, he brought them to conversion.

You, too, as time goes on, will progress in the ways of righteousness. Be happy about those who can break bad habits at once. But if you cannot, and you find yourself slipping back into the old habit patterns, do not despair!

For the rest of your life, you must realize that you depend more on Christ's repairing your wrongs than on your not committing them in the first place. We are all men and seem to learn only from the errors which we commit.

*   *

*

Be careful not to fall into the sin of pride! It is easy to become proud when you are crowned together with Jesus. St. Augustine writes: "Every other kind of evil is wrought by the doing of bad things. But it is the peculiar feature of pride, that it ruins even good deeds".

God will take infinite pains to keep your soul humble. Thank Him for this!

Having put aside pride, the Christian is not critical of other men. Shakespeare wrote: "I will chide no breather in the world than myself against whom I know most faults".

Try to be good, avoiding that kind of conventional goodness which is negative, censorious, narrow and altogether despicable.

*   *

*

It is sometimes the duty of a Christian to oppose other men. But he should weigh their faults without putting his thumb on the scales.

Sometimes a Christian even has to take part in armed fights, as for instance when his fatherland calls him. But he does not do it with a haughty spirit. Executioners in the Middle Ages did not execute someone without first begging his pardon. They knew themselves to be sinners punishing fellow-sinners. The murderer of Mahatma Gandhi first bowed to him, showing him his respect. It is only in this spirit that a Christian is allowed to criticize and to fight.

He always casts his nets on the right side, which in the

97

Bible symbolizes the side of clemency. You catch more fish with meekness than with harshness.

*　　*

*

A Christian has humility as his boat and flexibility as his chariot. To use Shakespeare's words in "As You Like It", a Christian "translates the stubbornness of fortune in a quiet and sweet style". He recognizes in what the world calls "justified indignation", the shine of satanic wisdom.

Against what are you righteously indignant? Against the sins of men? Sins of what gravity and of what number? Are they more and heavier than yours? There exists a God who must reserve for you eternal punishment if you do not forgive. What would you choose if you had to decide this very moment between forgiving and going into hell? Decide, with this in view! You will decide for meekness.

*　　*

*

I will share with you three thoughts which may help you to keep humble.

First, the thought about the unimportance of mankind.

A professor at the University of Moscow said to a Western Christian colleague: "I find it difficult to accept your faith in God's concern for human beings. Why did we have to wait so long if God really cared so much for the individual? Why were there all those thousands and millions of years before human life began? Why did God create man only on the sixth day? He seems not to have been in a hurry!"

The answer is simple. Before there were men, God loved the sun and the flowers and the animals. God did not plant cork trees to provide stoppers for our wine bottles, but because God loves the cork tree. He saw all that he had done, and behold, it was good. God walked through the garden of Eden planted by Him before there was an Adam and Eve. He could enjoy the fragrance of the lilies and the beauty of the roses.

The second thought is about your own unimportance.

Before going to prison, I had considered myself an important person. I was pastor of a growing church, author of books. I worked for the World Council of Churches, I was involved in charitable actions, and so on and so on. I could not imagine how all the church work in Romania would manage without me. When I came out after fourteen years of prison, I saw that the church had progressed very well without me, that others had written better books than mine. I had not been as necessary as I had considered myself to be.

This might be true in your case, too.

The third thought is about the importance of your brother.

Clement of Alexandria wrote, "He who sees his brother, sees God". This view puts you at once far below every fellow Christian with whom you might disagree. See the Godhead in him and bow with respect, even if he should be the frailest Christian. He is the master, you are the slave. Some theologians believe that Lucifer's fall lay in his refusal to be a ministering angel for men. He had replied haughtily: "Non serviam" (I do not serve).

*　　　*

*

The Christian speaks little. Nature has given us one tongue and two ears. Let the Christian eliminate his idle words and use his tongue to praise the Creator of his two ears.

*　　　*

*

I know that much of what is written above is only common sense. But common sense is not very common. And every ounce of religion requires ten pounds of common sense to apply it.

*　　　*

*

But do not be so meek as to give up the fulfilling of your aim. We see in the parable of the pounds (Luke 19) that the Lord Jesus does not make the attaining of His goals dependent on the consent of men. He likens Himself to a nobleman who receives his kingdom from the ruler of a far country, not from the votes of his fellow citizens. These latter hated him. Some of his servants were slothful. He slays his enemies that refused his reign. He must reign because he is the supreme good. To the measure that you identify yourself with him, you will be firm, that your faith may prevail at all costs (Gal. 1 :8–9).

*　　*

*

Your life should be Christ. Jesus had nowhere to lay His head. You may have a house, but only as a necessity, not as an indication of your desire to possess.

Birds from Alaska caged in the San Diego Zoo always look northward. So we look heavenward, to our true home.

*　　*

*

A Christian has one great guiding principle : it is love. We have to love our neighbour, to love him even when he steals our time, when he borrows and does not return, when he says bad words behind our back.

A Christian loves thus, without asking for love in exchange. George Bernard Shaw distinguishes between Christianity and Crosstianity, by which he means forcing on others a sadistic moralism. The whole Christian ethic is a code of rules only for us. Pliny the Younger wrote about the first Christians "how much they love each other".

*　　*

*

Wherever possible, prefer a competition in love to a quarrel with hatred.

Do not spend the few days of your short earthly life as a busybody meddling in the affairs of others, unless a common good is involved. Do not allow your attention to be distracted from Christ.

Accept the simple fact that some do not sympathize with you. This is normal. That you do not act according to their will can be a source of joy for you.

Avoid personal enmities as much as possible. "Make to yourselves friends," says Jesus (Luke 16 :9). Never break a friendship even for a sincere reason. No motive for breaking it is more important than a friendship.

*   *
*

The queen of Saba came to visit king Solomon and told him : "Your wisdom is world renowned. Allow me to see how you judge the people". So the next day two thrones were set up in the palace yard and the parties which had quarrelled were summoned to appear.

The first were two Jews, each with his hand in the other's beard, kicking and shouting the worse insults at each other. After the servants had parted them, the king asked what the fight was all about.

One said : "O King, I sold to this rascal two acres of land and he paid me the money for it. With this the question was settled. But on the next day he digged deep in the newly bought earth and found there an enormous treasure in gold and jewels. It was surely his, because I had sold to him the earth with everything it contained. It was my fault that I had not found the treasure before selling the land. But just imagine, this crook coming to me and saying : 'Dear brother, you were mistaken to sell me that field for nothing at all. Restore to me the money I gave you. The treasure is yours and take back your land also.' He would like me to cancel the bargain and afterward be punished by God for injustice, because I have no title-deed at all for either the land or the treasure. It had been a definitive sale",

And the man shouted to the other Jew : "You deceiver! The treasure is yours".

The king asked the other party to speak out. He begged : "Lord, have pity on my soul. I have bought only a piece of land, nothing more. I did not buy a treasure. I cannot keep a treasure worth millions for a few silver mines, which I paid as the price of the land. It would be unfair and I wish to be able to look in the eyes of God as an honest man. Tell this man that the treasure is his and only his!"

The queen of Saba could not believe her ears.

101

The king asked the first Jew, "Do you have any children?" He replied, "An eighteen-year-old daughter". He asked the other, "And you?" "I have a boy of twenty". The king gave the sentence: "The boy will marry the girl, and the treasure will be their dowry". The two parties embraced each other. The court case was finished.

The queen said: "I have never seen such a dispute in which each party says the other is right. How is it that such things happen with you?" The king answered: "But don't you know that we are the chosen people of God? We are a holy nation, which means that we have big quarrels, but all because the one esteems the other higher than himself, and every Jew would like his neighbour to be right in all differences. Is it not so with you? What would have happened if such a case had arisen in your country?"

The queen answered: "Everyone would have shouted, 'Mine is the treasure!'" Solomon asked: "And how would you have settled the dispute?" The queen was prompt in her reply: "I would have cut off the heads of both and taken the treasure for myself". The king asked again: "Do you have dogs and cats in your country?" The queen said: "Surely! Why do you ask?" Solomon finished the discussion with these words: "It is only for your pets that the sun still shines in your empire. God does not send the sun upon men who shout that they are right".

*   *

*

We have it from St. Anthony the Great that the only way to know God is through goodness.

Popular legend says that the wise men who came to worship the baby Jesus were three: Melchior, Balthasar and Gaspar. But the story is told that there were four. The name of the fourth was Artaban. Seeing the star which announced the birth of the Saviour, he had sold everything and had bought three very precious stones, a ruby, a sapphire and an emerald, to bring as gifts.

But while hurrying to the place where he was to meet the

three others for the journey to Palestine, he saw on the highway a man who had been robbed and beaten almost to death. He took him to an inn and gave the innkeeper the sapphire to cover expenses. The man he saved was a Jew, knowledgeable in the Scriptures. On learning of the purpose of his journey, he gave him his blessings and told him that the Messiah whom he went to greet was to be born in Bethlehem.

Artaban arrived at the meeting place too late. The other wise men had already left. So he travelled alone and came to Bethlehem. Here he was told that in truth a mysterious babe had been born in a stable not long before, that angels had sung at his birth, but that his parents had fled with him to an unknown destination.

Artaban rested from his journey at the home of a poor widow, mother of an only child. Suddenly at midnight, a neighbour rushed into the house and in tears said that the soldiers of Herod had killed her son and were slaughtering all the children in town. Artaban instructed the widow not to move. He went out of the house, locking the door behind him. When he saw an officer with drawn sword approaching, he met him with the ruby and said, "You can have this if you leave the house undisturbed. I live in it and I have no child". The officer, greedy, took the precious stone and went on his way.

The wise man comforted himself with the thought that he had at least one jewel left to offer to the newborn king of the Jews.

Over thirty years passed and Artaban could not find the One he sought. Finally he heard that He was living in Palestine, a prophet and doer of good deeds. Since Artaban had sought Him everywhere else, he turned eagerly toward Jerusalem. To his dismay, he was told when he arrived that the one born in Bethlehem was being led to Golgotha to be crucified, because he had called Himself the Son of God.

Artaban hurried to Calvary, knowing Him to be truly the Son of God because he had seen His star. The ageing wise man had one jewel left. Perhaps he could ransom Him by giving the precious stone to the executioners.

But on his way he passed through a slave market. A young girl begged those passing by, "Free me! I believe in Jesus. My religion teaches purity and I am to be sold to a life of shame and sin". Artaban sighed and said, "Forgive me, Son of God, but I have to give away even the last jewel that I had reserved for you". He ransomed this girl.

At once, darkness covered the earth. There was a great earthquake. The house where Artaban took shelter fell and buried him under its ruins. Dying, he begged the Son of God to forgive him for having given away everything to men and not to him. At the last moment, he heard a voice telling him : "Whatsoever you have done to these little brethren and sisters of mine, you have done unto me. Come and inherit the Kingdom which the Father has prepared for you from the beginning of the world". And so Artaban died.

* *
*

One thing is sure : Lenin loved mankind. He loved it so much that he would have been able to kill all men for the good of mankind, because mankind was for him an abstraction.

Jesus teaches a personal love for one's neighbour.

When missionaries wanted to translate the New Testament into the Mireba language of New Guinea, they found no word for love. So they used "Nanumangund", which means, "I give you my inner parts". Let our love be such.

And let us always remember that the soul of love is love for souls.

* *
*

Love is the distinctive feature of all Christians. From a pastor, especially, burning love is expected.

The story is told that St. John Chrysostom once went to a remote part of his diocese that suffered much from the absence of priests. There he instructed a peasant as best as he could and ordained him. After returning to his see in Constantinople,

104

he could not be quiet. "Have I not committed a mistake to install as priest somebody so unprepared for the ministry?" So he travelled back to that place and planned to arrive at the church a few minutes after the service had started. He hid himself behind a column to see how this peasant priest fulfilled his duty. Tears streamed from his eyes. He had never before seen a priest praying with so much devotion and such a glowing face, putting so much fervour in his short allocution and so gripping the hearts of all those present as he lifted them to heaven. When the liturgy was finished, St. Chrysostom entered the vicinity of the altar, knelt down before the priest, and asked for his blessing. The priest was shocked to see the bishop and said, "It is for you to bless me". The bishop insisted : "You bless me, because I have never before seen a priest serving God with so much fire and love in his heart". The ignorant priest, wondering, asked, "But, brother bishop, is it possible to serve God otherwise?"

*   *

*

God expects no better than to be vanquished by the loving look in your eyes. But men will resent your power. Spiritfilled Christians are hated. Great trees give more shade but also suffer stronger winds. But the arrows of hate aimed at you will never hit you, because you bear the shield of faith and you belong to another world which these arrows cannot reach.

Men will be able to inflict upon you only outward suffering. And even this you will recognize as coming ultimately by the will of your strange God, from whom you have decided to accept everything. Even an Auschwitz or a Buchenwald, burning ovens or gas chambers, will never succeed in making a Christian abandon his belief in God or his love for Him.

Nobody, not even God, has a club great enough to drive me away from Him. I will love Him though He slay me.

Believe in Christ and love. This is enough. Do not accept any extras—dogmas, rituals, rules, conditions attached by different organizations—as of primary importance.

Just love. Love even if you are not loved in return.

Jesus taught that when you are slapped you should turn the other cheek. The probable result will be a second and a third slap. I had the experience myself. A meek attitude is interpreted as weakness by the adversary. Christians in concentration camps would seek to fulfil the commandment of the Lord: when compelled to walk one mile with some heavy loads on their shoulders, they would walk two. The result was that the norm was increased next day and the exhausted prisoners had to fulfil tasks which crushed their bodies. Jesus told us to walk the extra mile. He never promised that this would give us success in our enterprises, but only that we would become perfect in love. This is enough.

*　　　*

*

This rule of simply fulfilling commandments without expecting any benefit beyond the perfection of Christian character applies also to other spheres of Christian life.

We have to bring the good news about Christ to other people. What reception we will get is not our business.

The story is told of a ship that sounded an SOS out on the stormy waters. The rescue crew immediately began to make preparations to take to sea.

One of the young lads spoke up: "Captain, don't you think these waters are too rough and the winds too fierce for us to go?"

The captain said, "No, the orders have come to go. There is a ship in distress. We must go".

The lad objected: "But, captain, we may not come back".

The captain replied, "Young fellow, we have not been commanded to come back, we have been commanded to go".

*　　　*

*

Accept injustice with satisfaction and joy.

The Jews have a joke. A man cried in a railway station, "Rubinstein! Rubinstein!" A Jew put his head out of the window. The man who had shouted gave him a slap, saying,

"Here you have what you deserve, you miserable Rubinstein". All in the compartment began to laugh. The slapped Jew also laughed, wholeheartedly. The other passengers asked him: "Why do you laugh?" He answered, "Well, I deceived him. I am not Rubinstein".

Gladly accept the kicks and slaps deserved by others and rejoice that somebody has been mistaken in hurting you instead of another. Jesus gave Himself to be beaten and killed in our place, for our sins.

During the socialist persecution of religion in Mexico in the Thirties, high prices were put on the heads of fugitive Catholic priests.

A Judas explained to a priest that he had always been poor. "By selling you," he said, "I could get some money and would have something to live on with my family." The priest left the forest where they had met and went with him to town, that Judas might sell him and give a piece of bread to his children. The priest was shot.

*   *

*

Thieves stole from a church during the religious service. Observing them, the abbot said to the monks: "Look how well they do their work. Let us do ours as well: let us pray for their salvation". And he continued the liturgy. The robbers left with their spoil.

*   *

*

Though love end with defeat for the lover, it is still the best of ways. But sometimes it can be victorious.

An English sergeant once stationed in Egypt tells this incident about himself: "There was a civilian in the same company who was converted. We gave that fellow an awful time. One very wet night, he came in tired. Before getting into bed, he went down on his knees to pray. My boots were heavy with wet mud, and I let him have one on each side of his head. He just went on with his prayers. Next morning, I found those boots beautifully polished and standing by the side of my bed.

That was his reply to me, and it broke my heart. I was saved that day".

* *

*

Stick to the Bible. Do not give a penny to any criticism of it, however scholarly it may be. Do not criticize the Bible, but let yourself be criticized by it.

In an exhibit of modern art, there was an empty canvas instead of a painting. Below it was the title, "A cow grazing". A visitor asked the artist, "What does this title mean? I see no grass. Where is the cow grazing?" The artist answered, "Well, the cow has eaten up all the grass". The visitor persisted : "But where is the cow?" The painter replied, "Why should the cow have remained if there was no grass left?"

Bible critics are like this artist. They leave in the Holy Scriptures only empty pages. No God, no miracles, no true history, no reliable teachings, no devil, no hell, and no paradise. Do not pay any attention to such artists!

St. John Chrysostom said : "We bid you believe the Scriptures. If any one agrees with the Scriptures, he is the Christian".

* *

*

If you study it attentively, you will surely find contradictions in the Bible. I mistrust stories which hold together in every detail. They are artificially construed. Believe in the Bible *because* the stories do not match.

* *

*

Do not be concerned about the scepticism of some scientists regarding the Bible. How much do scientists know? In one of Balzac's novels, a scientist, unmoved by his wife's weeping, says : "What are tears? I have analysed them. There is some phosphate of lime, chloride of soda, some mucus and some water". The one who looks at the Bible with such a distorted

108

mind is doomed not to understand it. You believe every letter of the Bible.

*　　　*

*

Beware of bigotry! Do not force others to have the same belief as yours. Rabindranath Tagore said rightly: "Bigotry tries to keep truth safe in the hand with a grip that kills it".

A Christian is tolerant with everybody, even with the intolerant.

*　　　*

*

An atheist lecturer proved that the Bible is not reliable. He opened to Ecclesiastes 1 :9, where it is written, "There is no new thing under the sun". Mockingly, he said, "This is an obvious lie. There are so many new things under the sun— X-rays, radio, cable, railways! So many inventions about which mankind had no idea centuries ago".

A Christian replied unperturbed. "The Bible is right, every iota of it. There is nothing new under the sun". Now the infidel got angry. "How can you be so stubborn and give such a stupid answer?" And he began to enumerate again the X-rays, the radio, railways, and so on.

The Christian's reply was: "Since the beginning, believers have said to unbelievers: 'You cannot deceive God with outward religion. God looks at the heart'. The unbelievers were sure of themselves: God cannot see the heart because it is covered with flesh and bones and skin. It is well hidden. So God asked Rontgen to make X-rays, with the help of which even we, men, can see inward parts. But they are not something new. They are modern illustrations of a truth which we believers have known for thousands of years".

The unbeliever had not expected this. He asked, "And what about radio?" "Old," was the immediate reply, "old as mankind itself. From the beginning, the faithful have said to those who lived in sin, 'Be careful in your speaking! God hears every word'. But the infidels have only replied in scorn, 'Heaven is

109

so far away. I cannot hear a debate going on in the next room. How can God in His distant heaven hear my words, especially the bad ones I pronounce in whisper?' So God ordered Marconi to construct a radio, which makes it possible for the people of London to hear even the cough of a speaker in Moscow. It all helps to awaken our souls to eternal truth. You do not see the one who lectures over the radio. He is far away. So God in heaven can hear every word of yours."

The infidel was at his wits' end. "Can you also show me that railways are not new?" "Surely! We have always warned, 'Repent today! Tomorrow it might be too late'. People delayed their repentance. So God arranged to have Stevenson create the railway. In order to avoid collisions, every train has to leave on the minute. If you arrive one minute too late, the train will have disappeared before your eyes—a good example of the old truth that the time for repentance is always now. You can have a heart attack the next minute."

Thus the Atheist lecturer said that there is no joking with this book.

The Bible is true, every letter is true. It is true even in its contradictions.

*   *

*

Stick to prayer. Heaven and earth can be in as direct communication as London and Berlin. Only make your prayer a radical decision between you and God.

*   *

*

Never pray as to a God who is unwilling to give. Seneca wrote: "The gods are not like men. They give and give to others until they leave themselves bare".

*   *

*

Unanswered prayer does not exist. During the last war, Christians in both Germany and Britain prayed for victory. The unanswered prayers of the Germans were an answer to the prayers of the British. We live in a world divided into nations,

110

races, classes, parties, religions and conflicting individual interests. Why must your interest always prevail with God? If after having prayed for a victory you are defeated, be happy! It means that your adversaries' prayers have been accepted by God. He is still a God who hears prayer.

*   *

*

Let your life be one of service.

Do not say that you have no spiritual power or qualifications. A boy gave to Jesus five loaves of bread and two fish. Jesus multiplied them. But what if the boy had had nothing? Such a possibility does not exist. In the Bible, the word "zero" or its mathematical symbol "0" never occurs. The Bible is constructed mathematically. Every letter of the Hebrew and Greek alphabet corresponds with a figure. Every word has a numerical value. My son has written his thesis for the B.D. degree at the Lutheran University of Paris on the subject of mathematics in the Bible. But the Bible contains neither the word "zero" nor the sign for it "0", which is especially significant when you realize that the Chaldean ancestors of the Jews already had the zero written as a circle. The very word "zero" comes from the Chaldean "zer".

Nobody is a zero before God. Nobody is without some gift. Your gift is perhaps the humility to believe that you have none.

*   *

*

On May 21, 1972, I had a vision in St. Stephen's Church in Southport, Great Britain. I meditated kneeling before the altar. I remembered that Elijah had asked a widow for a piece of bread. The woman answered that she had very little flour and oil left, just enough for one last meal for her son and herself (1 Kings 17:11–12).

At once, I had before my eyes a hungry man, begging bread from the Virgin Mary. She answered: "I have none. I am a mother of sorrows and my Son was hanged on a cross. There He cried that He was forsaken even by God. Bread I have not,

111

but I can give you the comfort of knowing that it is worth-while to endure all things for God".

This hungry man became a zealous preacher and made thousands nourish Jesus with adoration.

*　　*

*

Never complain about your cross.

A Christian once complained to God about it. So God took him to His storehouse and told him, "You are free to choose whatever cross you like". One was beautiful, golden, but very heavy; another light but rugged and apt to wound one's shoulder. In the end he found in the corner a cross which he thought would suit him. God said to him, "Have a better look at it". It was the cross which he had first received from God.

Suffering is sacred. Never squander as much as the smallest crumb of it!

*　　*

*

Know God, but know also the devil.

"The Pastor Hermas," an ancient Christian book, says that every man has a personal devil haunting him, as he has a personal guardian angel. Try to know well the angel, who is your bodyguard. Try to know well your devil, too.

*　　*

*

There exists a dangerous fashion among some youngsters today. The moment they are converted, they drop their jobs and studies in order to become preachers. This antagonizes their families. Running after others, whom they most probably will never win to Christ, they lose the possibility of bringing salvation to their relatives. Remain in your place and win your own family for Christ, if you can.

To be a missionary is a rare and exceptional vocation.

The truer a Christian is to Christ, the greater is the likelihood that he will live in intellectual and spiritual isolation.

This does not mean that he will not be a missionary. He

will be one of a special kind. You do not have to force water down the mountainside into the valley. It flows by itself. Missionary work is not done strenuously. Exist on a high level and the word of God will pour down upon those below you. I appreciate missionary work. There is something wrong in missionary effort.

*   *

*

In the Louvres is the painting "The Miracle of San Diego" by Murillo. Two noblemen and a priest enter a kitchen. They are amazed that all kitchenmaids are angels. One handles a pot, another a joint of meat, still another a basket of vegetables and one tends the fire. But they all do angelic work.

No labour is common unless we make it so. Jesus Himself, the One with the greatest mission, worked in a woodshop. Please, unless you have a very clear, exceptional call, do not become a missionary in the professional sense of the word! Rather, be a missionary in your kitchen or factory. You will be more useful there.

*   *

*

But never lose the broader prospective. Care for the evangelizing of the world. Care also for social justice.

The Lord Jesus told a parable about a prodigal son who wasted his father's substance with riotous living. After many adventures, he returned to his father, who received him with love, fed him with the fatted calf, gave him good garments and even placed on his finger a golden ring.

This prodigal son now enjoyed himself, and that was all.

The Lord warned us not to seek the truth in His parables. The parables are for those who cannot take in the truth.

Normally, a youngster who had done such things would have to think about restitution to his father and about trying to win for God his former comrades in revelry and wickedness. He also could have eaten a little bit less of the fatted calf and cared about the inhabitants of a hungry country in which he had lived for a while.

H

A Christian thinks about all these things, which means that he gets involved in evangelistic and social problems. But he has no illusions about perfecting society before the return of the Lord Jesus. Do your duty to witness for Christ and to improve society, but be temperate in all things. Do not over-do. Overwork is a drug for the disappointed, and revolutions are the worst opium for the people.

Keep the right balance between a small life of self-interest and an exaggerated desire to bring about the immediate con-version of mankind or the establishing of justice, which take generations to accomplish.

*   *
*

For centuries there has been a war against poverty. But there is more poverty in the world today than ever before. For centuries men have talked of disarmament or the abolition of war, yet in Vietnam alone more bombs have been dropped than were used against Germany in the whole World War II. We try to fill the gap between generations. In the museum of antiquity in Constantinople, there is the oldest piece of writing known to men. It bears the following inscription: "Alas times are not what they used to be! Children no longer obey their parents, and everybody is writing a book about it".

It is a utopian dream to force a caterpillar to be a chrysalis, or a chrysalis to be a butterfly. It is a utopian dream to plan a good social state for unrighteous men.

It is a hard thing for a Christian to see demons triumph over nations. But the best remedy is to enter into quietness and say to yourself: "We have no solution for the social prob-lems of mankind, just as we have no solution for the squaring of the circle".

*   *
*

At the root of all social and racial unrest is the trespassing against the tenth commandment: "Thou shalt not covet". Why do you need more than you have?

114

I wonder if there are many who have experienced as much hunger and destitution as I have. For a long time, my ration of food was one slice of bread a week and daily a soup of dirty potato peels. I had neither shoes nor trousers. I trembled for cold. You can be happy even under such conditions. You can be happy even while knowing that your wife, too, suffers the same hardship and your child is deprived of all the joys of life. This is what your mysterious, heavenly Father has allotted you, and that is it.

I know that voluntary poverty is one thing: a poverty imposed upon you by exploiters is something else. You have to oppose the latter. But in order to oppose it successfully, you must have power.

You are never so influential as when you are really quiet. You do not seem mighty, but that not-seeming is part of the quality. Live in eternity, not in daily incidents and the succession of events. Eternity cannot be disturbed even by the cry of a million hungry children. If you are seated serenely in heavenly places, what you do for these hungry children will bring fruit. Otherwise your whole fight will be just vanity. It will be like Sysiphus rolling a huge stone uphill: each time it falls back he has to roll it up again. The whole of human history has been like this. That which stands has been accomplished by the quiet spirits, by those who are above the intermittent bubbles called centuries with their transitory sufferings and joys.

The world is not just a garden, a wonderful creation, as some religious hymns say. There is an ugly side to it. It will be overcome by the fierce fight of the quiet. The still small voice prevails.

*　　　*

*

Even the ungodly accomplish very good things through social fights, reforms, revolutions and war. Only that these will not last.

There were once two boy silkworms who raced for the love of a girl silkworm and ended up in a tie.

115

This is also the end of all social struggles. The fighters on both sides become clay.

*   *
*

The Tibetan ascetic Milarepa had kept for himself only a pot from which to drink water. One day it broke. Then Milarepa said:

My earthly pot now is and now is not.
My sole possession—
By breaking, it has become a lama.
For it has preached an admirable discourse
On the impermanence of things.

Dedicate yourself to your soul. Others will come to salvation by the contagious force of a faithful character. As for human society, leave it to the One who bears the responsibility for it.

"Except the Lord build the house, they labour in vain that build it. Except the Lord keep the city, the watchman wakes but in vain. It is vain for you to rise up early, to sit up late, to eat the bread of sorrows". (Psalm 127:1–2.)

Three times—"in vain".

Surely, many things have to be done in society. But from Livingstone, the great fighter against slavery and the great missionary and explorer, we have the word, "Whosoever has faith is not in haste".

*   *
*

We are not in haste because we believe in our immortality. Many things which are not achieved now will be achieved later. Moses pleaded with God to enter the Holy Land. God refused him. He had to die outside of it. Some two thousand years pass. The Lord Jesus speaks on Mount Tabor with Moses. Tabor is in Palestine, which means that the desire of Moses has been fulfilled notwithstanding, though a little bit later. What are two thousand years to one who lives eternally?

"Always be true to your immortality," wrote Solzhenitsyn. Then people will be able to say about you what Goethe said about Lavater: "In his vicinity, you become virginal".

*   *

*

Why do some people riot? There are many motivations. Among others is the fact that rebellion is one of the greatest of human pleasures. Many consider it a higher pleasure than sex, alcohol, music or drugs.

During the disorders in Belfast, the number of suicides decreased by fifty per cent. The number of persons treated by physicians for depression also decreased. Aggressiveness against one's neighbour diminishes that against oneself. For those who do not have worthwhile tasks to engage their energies, social peace or peace between nations and races is boresome.

There is also in every rebellion an element of exasperation. Wild crowds do not care much if things are better, provided they will be different. They exchange flies for bumble bees and bees for hornets. Revolutions change the social order, but they rarely improve it.

Sun-Yat-Sen, who started the Chinese revolution that has continued for sixty years, wrote towards the end of his life: "If we analyze our first promptings to carry out the Chinese revolution, we shall see that we had in view the salvation of the Chinese people and the country, whereas the result has been quite the opposite, and the Chinese people are becoming more and more oppressed, the country more and more unhappy".

*   *

*

For these and many other reasons, real Christians have always opposed rioters, guerrillas and the like.

When the peasant troubles started in Germany during the Reformation, Luther first wrote "Advice for Peace". But when the events became violent, he wrote a pamphlet "Against the Murderous Rioting Bands of Peasants". He condemned them in the strongest possible terms as rebels against God and their rightful lords. He called for their suppression. When the rebellion had been suppressed, he interpreted the event as a righteous judgment of God.

*   *
*

Know all this! Do not enter easily into battle. But if you are forced to do battle, be prepared to win.

You will regret bitterly every weakness in your fight. When Danton attacked the Tuileries, Louis XVI did not permit his troops to defend the palace, that blood might not be shed. He took refuge in the National Assembly. The result was that more blood was shed than if he had defended his authority. Danton's rebels killed everybody in the palace, starting with the marshal and finishing with the cook. The corpses were maimed. Then followed the reign of terror, to which even Danton fell victim.

*   *
*

Shakespeare wrote in "As You Like It" that "Love is to be made of sighs and tears, of faith and service, fantasy, all made of passion and all made of wishes; all adoration, duty and observance, all humbleness, all patience and impatience, all purity, all trial, all obeisance". There is more to love than this. Love for the French people should have obliged Louis Ludovic XVI to fight to the uttermost against the rebels.

Let us be sure that our fierce fighting proceeds from love.

*   *
*

Church Fathers living in the desert discussed, after decades of prayer and fasting, which is the highest Christian virtue. The one said "love", the other "righteousness", the third "austerity", the fourth "humility", and so on. St. Anthony the Great ended the debate with the words: "The highest virtue is to have in all things the right measure". All agreed.

*   *
*

After coming to Jesus, you will love His church, too. You will see His church with new eyes. There are many ugly and

118

repulsive things in the church, but like a seed it also contains much potential. The seed has within it the possibility of becoming a beautiful flower. So has even the most decayed church.

You cannot bear the sermons of the pastor? You consider them very bad?

As if to accustom us to poor and very wrong sermons, Jesus delivered a sermon which superficial Christians would consider bad. You find it in Matthew 15:23. He calls a woman a dog, only because she belongs to another nation. The sermon seems to be full of spirit of caste by saying that Jews are the children and that the food reserved for them should not be given to dogs. But this sermon, which we would consider bad, is the black background on which is painted the beautiful deed of healing the sick daughter of that woman and of teaching her humility.

Could it be that the bad sermons of pastors are meant to teach you humility and to remind you how often your own words are bad? In any case, unbearable sermons are the output of an institution that for two thousand years has kept before mankind the remembrance of the one who deserves our whole love, our Lord Jesus Christ.

Learn from weak and bad sermons. Balaam set an example of humility. He was ready to listen even to an ass when it told him in very plain language a truth from God.

You complain about the preacher. There might be something wrong with the listener, too.

*   *

*

Learn to distinguish between the true church and institutions which only bear the name. The one who gave a definitive status to the church state from which most of the major denominations derive, the emperor Theodosius, slaughtered the whole male population of Thessaloniki. The biography of Constantine the Great is horrible.

Clovis, king of the Francs, became a Christian because he loved the Christian princess Clotilde. He promised during a battle that he would take her God as his God, if he conquered the Allemans. His victory was hardly sufficient reason to accept the Christian faith, according to which Francs should not fight against Allemans, but live in peace with them. The people accepted Christianity because the king ordered it.

Duke Vladimir of Kiev became a Christian in order to marry the Byzantine princess Anne. He forced the whole of Russia to become Christian.

When Finland was defeated by the Swedes under St. Eric, the people were compelled to embrace Christianity.

There have been some very bad popes and many bad bishops as well as many good ones. But often offerings heaped upon the altar of the apostles went straight into the pockets of the clergy.

Pope Julius who built St. Peter's dome in Rome was a man of war.

Pope Leo X, who excommunicated Luther, is reported to have said: "What profit has not the fable of Christ brought us!"

When Protestantism separated from Catholicism, peace was settled after many wars on the principle "Cuius regio, eius religio", which means that people everywhere had to follow the religion of their prince.

A church created and perpetuated in such a manner could only be unfaithful to Christ. We tell about the authority of this church what Samuel said to king Saul: "Thou hast rejected the word of the Lord and the Lord has rejected thee" (1 Samuel 15:26).

Luther and Melanchthon regretted that they had reformed too much. Melanchthon wrote in 1530: "Oh, if I could reestablish not the worldly, but the spiritual administration of the church through bishops, because I see what a church we will have after the dissolution of church order and discipline". Luther wrote to Melanchthon: "I think we have gone too far in the good". I, on the contrary, regret that the reformers did not go far enough.

The Reformed churches have been intolerant toward the

preaching of the true gospel just as the Catholic church had been before them. The Church of England had no place for either Bunyan or Wesley when they were alive. Today, there are commemorative plates for them in Westminster Abbey, centuries after their death.

The Reformed churches as well as the Catholic and the Orthodox (except under atheist or non-Christian regimes) are identical with the world. Everybody is baptized as an infant and everybody is a Christian. The world cannot accept the whole Christ. Neither can such a church.

She can only misuse money entrusted to her, as the world does. We read in II Kings 12, that bricklayers were more trusted in money matters than priests. Things have not changed since.

Wycliffe wrote: "If the priesthood misuses church treasures, they must be taken from it. Otherwise, you neglect your duty". And Bonnhoffer: "The church is a church only when she exists for others. To begin with, she must give away all her property to the needy. Pastors must live only on the free will offerings of believers. If necessary, they must exercise a secular profession".

Thinking about the nominal church, Paul Tillich wrote: "The first word to be spoken by religion to the people of our time must be a word spoken against religion".

He expresses in other words what we find already in *The Sum of Theology,* written by Thomas Aquinas: "When there is an imminent danger for faith, prelates can be accused even publicly by their subordinates".

*　　*

*

In this false church, the word "Christian" can strike terror to the heart. Christians have done to Christians as much harm, in as cruel a manner, as Nazis or Communists or other pagans have done. Not every man you consider a Christian *is* a Christian.

*　　*

*

But the word "church" also has another sense. By becoming a Christian, you will enter into a real fellowship of brethren and sisters in the faith.

Nobody counterfeits what is not valuable. The many counterfeits of Christianity prove its value. There are pretenders only to pure life, none to a bad one.

Leave the pretenders to Christianity and attach yourself to the true church. In it are some big saints, real poems of God. This is the Greek word which the Bible uses to describe them—"poema" (Eph. 2:10).

I agree with Pope Pelagius II that God cannot be on the side of a man who is not in peace and unity with the church, provided that we understand by "church" this sacred fellowship of cross-bearing real believers.

But be prepared to have disappointments here, too. God's true church consists of people who only strive towards godliness, without having reached it yet. Remember that you are also a disappointment to others.

Real Christians are also capable of treachery and cruelty.

Wicked men have virtues, saints have sins. The world is not divided into white and black. It will sometimes be difficult for you to distinguish between the true and the false.

St. Thomas Aquinas said: "Gratia non tollit naturam" (Grace does not destroy nature).

Beware especially when you receive many gifts from God. Graces and gifts can serve as enemies. They seldom provoke admiration. In most cases they provoke envy.

In spite of the weaknesses of its members, the church is real if it is a fellowship of believers and in it you are taught the Word of God.

*　　　*

*

But again: Do not have too great expectations!

In the Bible we have the word of God, but what an imprecise word. In Matthew 21:7, we read that the disciples brought to Jesus an ass and a colt, . . . and they set Him thereon, which gives the impression that they set Him on two animals. The word of God is written in part by uneducated man in an unpolished language.

When God became man, he became a despised man, counted among robbers. When he gave his written word, he gave it with many imprecise and obscure parts. When he gave us priests and pastors he knew we would be taught sermons and books containing much human ignorance and distortion.

At poor religious services, remember Jesus in His humility. The humble church is the extension of the humble incarnation.

*　　*
*

After having made this distinction between denominations as such and the real church, children of God must maintain unity. It is a shame that on Sundays we scatter to hundreds of confessions and often leave Him alone (John 16:32). The Greek word for "scatter" is "scorpithete" which is akin to "scorpions".

Apply to all brethren this principle: "In necessary things unity, in dubious things liberty, in all charity".

Very important is this unity. The last words of Melanchthon were: "Let them be one!" He had them from Jesus: ". . . that they all may be one".

Strive towards unity, but again without illusions. You will not achieve much. Confusion and discord shall spread more and more even among the children of God, like clouds of darkness. Even among believers it will be a problem to find a congregation and a pastor to satisfy the needs of your soul. Guard what you have already received and keep the faith in Christ, even if you have to hold unto the root of the tree by your fingernails to stop yourself from being swept away, and thus remain until the day of your death. A better world awaits you where clarity reigns.

*　　*
*

I spoke about faithfulness toward the church, but it must also be clear that we cannot be in communion with God

123

through the church and have at the same time a direct relationship with God. The church makes the relationship indirect. Liberty of conscience *vis-a-vis* God is greater than the authority of the church. The church has always found it difficult to identify the saints. She has sentenced and condemned many godly persons as heretics.

You must be aware that you run in vain if you do not run with the true church. But at the same time, you have to keep a certain distance even from the truest church.

*   *

*

Never allow yourself to be discouraged by things which you see in the church. The story is told of a Jew who was converted after having seen the Vatican during the time of Borgia. He said : "A church which exists in spite of such leaders must be with God".

I love the church mostly for its ugly sides. When you enter a hospital, you feel revulsion at the stench, pus, blood, groanings. This is the beauty of a hospital, that it receives sick men and that doctors and nurses are prepared to spend their days amid such unpleasant conditions in order to help. The beauty of the church consists in the fact that it receives sinners and criminals. After being received by the church, these sinners commit new wicked deeds, this time under the cloak of Christianity. And the church, a loving mother, continues to keep them at her loving bosom.

I find this beautiful.

And then there is also another side to the church. It contains not only wicked men.

It has men like Pope Gregory the Great who, while putting on liturgical garments, was told that a man had died for hunger. Immediately, he put aside the robes, saying, "If one man dies for hunger in Rome, the Pope is not worthy to say the mass".

The church has given and still gives a whole constellation of men who love God and their fellowmen wholeheartedly and put themselves at their service.

The church has a rich experience with God and with men. Its treasury is at your disposal.

Whatever happens in the church, good or evil, there remains one crucial fact! the resurrection of Jesus. It is surely true.

Suppose, as our adversaries say, that this whole story is forged: why would forgers invent the episodes in which Mary Magdalene does not recognize the resurrected Lord? According to Luke 24:16 and John 21:4, His closest disciples did not recognize Him to be Jesus. Imagine, if you will, that several persons plot to accuse a man falsely for a crime he did not commit and then, when they appear in the witness stand, each one says that he does not recognize the accused as having been the criminal. Obviously, their whole cause would collapse. Now, forgers are usually very intelligent men. If the apostles were forgers, why would they have repeated the stupidity, unforgivable for a forger, of saying that they did not recognize the person before them as the resurrected Jesus? The explanation is simple: because they were lovers of truth and things had happened just as they tell them. Jesus later gave signs enough to dispel every doubt in their heart. They knew that he was alive. So do we.

He is alive not only in heaven: He lives in our hearts. If your spiritual eyes are open and you look at a believer, you see Jesus enthroned in his heart, or, to change the figure, the believer himself lying at His bosom, safely wrapped in both arms of Jesus.

Cling always to the one sure fact: Jesus rose from the dead. He is alive. He has been dead, now what had happened to His corpse? Had His disciples stolen it? Then they would have known that He had not fulfilled His promise to rise again. They would assuredly have lost their faith. Almost all of them later died a martyr's death. No one goes to death under torture for what he himself knows to be a lie. So the corpse of Jesus was not in the hands of the disciples.

If it had been in the hands of His adversaries, Christianity would never have arisen. When the apostles preached the resurrection of Jesus, the chief priests who had sentenced Him to death would only have had to open the tomb and show the body of Jesus. The three thousand who were converted in one day in Jerusalem—a heavy blow indeed for the Pharisees—would never have accepted the claims of the resurrection had they seen the body of Jesus still lying in the tomb. Peter would easily have been humiliated and discredited if his claims about his resurrected Lord had been disproved.

Neither the friends nor the enemies of Jesus possessed His corpse because on the third day Jesus was no more a corpse, but alive. He is alive today and will be throughout eternity.

You might have tribulations in the world and within the church, but the living Jesus will give you joy amidst tribulation.

*   *

*

In fellowship with Jesus, how easy it will be for you to know the right Christian attitude toward the problems of your life.

In Dostoievski's *Brothers Karamazov,* the Great Inquisitor, on learning that a certain Jesus Christ was walking through the streets of Madrid and by his unwanted presence endangering the Christian religion which he had happened to found, summoned Jesus before him and lectured him on how foolish he had been. As an idealist and a utopian, Jesus could only have been crucified. It was men like the Great Inquisitor who have made Christianity persist by putting it in a fixed frame and burning those with the mind of Jesus.

To all the insolence and cruelty of the Great Inquisitor, Jesus never answered a word. He listened attentively to the end. Was it not a creature of God, a man for whom he had died, that spoke? When the Great Inquisitor had finished, Jesus kissed him. That was all.

Let a kiss be your final answer to any insolence and cruelty. Even Judas Iscariot desired the kiss of Christ.

*   *

*

You have to deal with men, to listen to them, to give them your replies. But leave them as quickly as you can. "One thing is needful," and Mary Magdalene chose "that good part": she sat quietly at Jesus' feet an heard His word. She needed only Jesus, even when He was crucified, yes, even when He was a corpse. She loved Him and only Him. And He loved her so much that He took great risks in accepting her kisses and loving gestures. In that time no rabbi would have allowed a woman even to touch him. For Jesus also only one thing is needful: to show love to Magdalene's.

The eyè by which she saw Jesus was the same as the eye by which Jesus saw her. There are many bodily eyes. The spiritual eye is one. It is common to God, the angels, and believers.

*   *

*

A shepherd said to a nightingale, "Sing!" The nightingale replied, "The frogs make too much noise. It takes away the pleasure of singing. Don't you hear them?" The shepherd said, "I surely do, but only your silence makes me hear them".

Walk through the world singing the song of Jesus. It is to your shame if so many words of hatred and unbelief are heard.

*   *

*

If you are faithful to Christ and to His church, when you finish your earthly life paradise will be honoured to receive you. But you have a higher calling than paradise and the heavenly Jerusalem. You are called to sit with Jesus on His throne, from which universes are created and ruled, just as Jesus has overcome and sits on the throne with His Father. (Revelation, 3:21.) Paradise will be for you just a time of relaxation. Divine tasks await you, because you will have become Christ-like, a partaker or the divine nature.

*   *

*

I have told you the word of God. It will help you if you listen to it.

I do not know if you will. But the present book has helped me.

Since I came to the West nine years ago, I have written tirelessly about the Communist persecution of Christians. It is now a long time since I came out of Communist prisons. But till now, Communist prisons had not come out of me.

A young patient of a psychotherapist painted dozens of women's faces cracked like broken vases, faded like worn flowers, and with hard, unyielding eyes. Only when he had painted a whole and healthy face did he know that he could be cured and that he was a painter.

For the first time, I have written a book the only subject of which is Christ. Through it I have been healed of having my mind burdened continually with Communism and its prisons.

*   *
*

For further information on other books
written by the Wurmbrand family,
please write:

Christian Missions to the Communist World Inc.
P.O. Box 938
Middlebury, IN   46540

Titza Mihalache
1510 164th St. #4
San Leandro, CA 94578